D1272751

THE HUMAN PAIR
IN THE WORK OF THOMAS HARDY

THE HUMAN PAIR
IN THE WORK OF
THOMAS HARDY

An Essay on the Sexual Problem
As treated in the Wessex Novels, Tales and Poems

By

PIERRE D'EXIDEUIL

TRANSLATED FROM THE FRENCH BY FELIX W. CROSSE
WITH AN INTRODUCTION BY HAVELOCK ELLIS

KENNIKAT PRESS
Port Washington, N. Y./London

THE HUMAN PAIR IN THE WORK OF THOMAS HARDY

First published in 1930
Reissued in 1970 by Kennikat Press
Library of Congress Catalog Card No: 79-105779
ISBN 0-8046-1012-6

Manufactured by Taylor Publishing Company   Dallas, Texas

To Monsieur FLORIS DELATTRE

59702

Love is a sowre delight, and sugred griefe,
A living death, and ever dying life.

Desperate Remedies.

The paths of love are rougher
Than thoroughfares of stones.

Time's Laughingstocks.

You should have taken warning,
Love is a terrible thing: sweet for a space
And then all mourning, mourning.

Human Shows.

CONTENTS

CONTENTS

INTRODUCTION

IT is common to speak of Thomas Hardy as a
"pessimist." It is not a description he himself
accepted. One may well go further and say that
for anyone who is concerned with the spectacle of
life the term "pessimism" is as much out of place
as the term "optimism." The person who believes
that everything in the world is for the best can only
have known one hemisphere of it and only have felt
half of what it offers; he is a maimed and defective
being who has never in any complete sense lived.
And the person who believes that everything in the
world is for the worst is similarly one-sided in his
vision, and semi-ignorant in his experiences. No one
indeed who has really caught a glimpse of the infinitely varied universe of experience in which we live
can apply to it such demoded metaphysical terms
as "optimism" and "pessimism." It is true, as a
distinguished French critic has lately remarked:
"Humanity does not give birth in joy, and even the
novelists most optimistic in their philosophy, like
André Gide, have yet written bitter things. The
great masterpieces of fiction reach us effaced by time
and commentaries, but think of the corrosive acid
that poisoned on their first appearance *Les Liaisons
Dangereuses* or *Le Rouge et Le Noir*. Nothing more
atrociously desperate than *The Mill on the Floss*, or
Le Cousin Pons or *The Possessed*." Jaloux is here

xiii

refuting the charge of " pessimism " brought against
the novels of Julien Green, but he might have been
speaking of Hardy or even of Shakespeare. For
Shakespeare no more becomes a pessimist by virtue
of *Lear* than an optimist by virtue of *Midsummer
Night's Dream*. The artist lifts us into a region
where these metaphysical distinctions are meaning-
less, and we may well feel sorry for the simple folk
who can turn from the radiant exhilaration of
Hardy's art and mutter " Pessimist ! "

It is another matter to say that life is a tragedy
and a comedy, and, often enough, both together.
There is an inescapable logic of sequences in it, and
there is a wild absurdity; there is anguish and there
is joy; there is, in the end, the serene contemplation
of a whole in which all the varied elements fall into
place. That is how those who approach life naturally—that is to say, unobsessed by philosophical
dogmas—inevitably feel, whether or not they happen
to be artists : as a tragedy, and also at times a farce,
a source of delight, sometimes of horror, even, sometimes, of irony, in short, as Dante phrased it, a
" divine comedy." Life has indeed always been so
for the natural man, from whatever Adam and Eve
you choose to trace him.

It was so that life was for Hardy. He interested
himself a little in philosophy, and more in art; as
the years went on he interested himself in fiction as
an art, his own in particular, and even wrote sug-
gestively about it. But, whether or not he was a
great artist, he was not a philosopher. He was a
natural and simple man as free from the pretentious-
ness of " high art " as from any other pretence, so
modest and human as to feel hurt by the clamour of

fools around his *Jude the Obscure*. Hardy was not a child of culture nor even, one sometimes thinks, a well-trained workman in literature. He had never been subjected to any discipline, scarcely, so far as one can see, even in architecture; his education was mainly the outcome of a random, inquisitive, miscellaneous reading, and the love-letters he wrote in youth to the dictation of unschooled peasant girls (like Richardson and like Restif de la Bretonne) may well have been an important part of it. His stories lapse at times into extravagance or absurdity. His style, exquisite at moments, is often (though this may be justified by his belief that " a living style lies in not having too much style—being in fact a little careless ") weak, feeble, careless. It is genius that carries him through. And of its possession he seemed mostly unconscious.

His modest, quiet, smiling simplicity was the dominant impression the man made, at all events in earlier days, when one met him. I only knew him slightly—a few meetings, an occasional letter—and my most vivid memory dates from a long afternoon spent alone with him as far away as some forty years, before he had become famous. (I had, not long before, in the *Westminster Review* for April, 1883, published an article on his novels which was one of the earliest serious appreciations of his work and my own earliest long essay.) Yet even so brief a meeting may suffice to furnish a key to a writer's work, and to reveal the quality of the atmosphere in which that work moves.

The tragi-comedy of life, its joy and its pain, most often have their poignant edge at the point of sex. That is especially so when we are concerned with a highly sensitive, alert, rather abnormal child of nature, with the temperament of genius. Such we in part know, in part divine, that Hardy was, though always reticent about any auto-biographical traits in his novels. Every reader of Mrs Hardy's *Early Life of Thomas Hardy* has noted the statement that " a clue to much in his character and action throughout his life is afforded by his lateness of development in virility, while mentally precocious. He himself said humorously in later times that he was a child till he was sixteen, a youth till he was five-and-twenty, and a young man till he was nearly fifty." The statement may be vague, but it indicates an element of abnormality such as we are apt to find in genius; some such element is indeed an inevitable concomitant of the special sensitiveness and new vision of genius,—the new vision of things seen at an angle slightly, yet significantly, different from that at which the average man is placed. For genius feels the things we all feel but feels them with a virginal freshness of sensation, a new pungency or a new poignancy, even the simplest things, the rustling of the wind in the trees or over the heather, which become, since Hardy has revealed them to us, an experience we had never before known.

It is in the problems of the relations of men and women that, as we might expect, these qualities of Hardy's special genius reach their full expression. That cannot fail to have been observed by all those who have discussed his work in fiction. But I doubt if it has ever been so thoroughly and so frankly discussed as in *Le Couple Humain dans l'Oeuvre de Thomas Hardy* by M. Pierre d'Exideuil, recently published in Paris and here presented to the English reader. He is the first writer to investigate Hardy's art in relation to the sexual theme at its centre. It is worth noting that this task falls to a fellow countryman of Stendahl and of Proust, and so many other fine analysts in love. The English critic still always remains rather shy and awkward, a little puritanical, in front of the problems of sex. There lingers in him a medieval feeling that to deal simply and seriously with sex is unwholesome. He seems to feel an impulse either to moralise or to display an ostentatious playfulness which sadly often becomes coarse and crude. Throughout the whole history of French literature, even from the days of Montaigne and *Petit Jehan de Saintre*, it has been natural for the Frenchman to deal seriously with a group of problems which certainly, for nearly all of us, are at one time or another the most serious we encounter in life. (I may note parenthetically that Hardy's characters are largely of the distinctly Celtic type of Western England, and that Hardy himself, who felt in close touch with the great French novelists, liked to recall that he was remotely of French blood.) M. d'Exideuil is dealing with a foreign writer, but he is following a track marked out by his own countrymen.

It is the business of the analytic critic to trace out the underlying tendencies, the more or less unconscious ideas, held beneath and within the work of art he is discussing. In so doing he may easily give the impression that the artist himself deliberately built up his work on the foundation of these tendencies, and intentionally used the ideas as the framework of his structure. That is not so; and certainly not so for an artist as spontaneous and wayward as Hardy, who used ideas and theories, by afterthought, as illustrations or decorations of his stories, not as their framework. The artist, we must never forget, is simply a man who looks at life through the medium of a personal temperament, and is able to describe what it looks like as seen by him. But the artist himself may not know what it looks like from outside. As Hardy once wrote to me : " They (novelists) are much in the position of the man inside the hobby-horse at a Christmas masque and have no consciousness of the absurdity of its trot, at times, in the spectator's eyes." It was not indeed any absurdity in my vision of his work that he was criticising but rather an appreciativeness which, he modestly said, " seems in many cases to create the beauties it thinks it perceives." The critic of literature, however, is in the same position as the grammarian of language. The grammarian patiently observes language and finds that certain rules hold good, in general, for its use. But the rules he evolves from observations of the common uses of language are not present to the minds of those who invented and spoke the language ; they come after, not before, its creation. And similarly, the rules the critic finds in the novelist's art, however justly they may define the general methods of that art, were not present to the artist's mind ; they come after, not before, the creation of that art. We must bear that in mind when M. d'Exideuil so lucidly expounds to us what he finds in Hardy's novels.

All those who have ever taken a real interest in Hardy's work will enjoy this intimate study of what cannot but be regarded as one of the most significant aspects of that work. But even those readers who take no special interest in Hardy's novels may yet find much that is profitable here. For here we are concerned with the central situations of life, stated in terms of fictional creation but none the less situations which most of us have had to deal with. The men whom Hardy brings before us have sometimes been criticised as rather pale and featureless in character. Many years ago I remarked that men of the Wilhelm Meister and Daniel Deronda class were his favourite heroes. He wrote in reply : " I think you are only saying in another way that these men are the modern man—the type to which the great mass of educated modern men of ordinary capacity are assimilating more or less." Evidently it was not on the same plane that he saw women. The problems of love he presents, therefore, are largely those of the conflict between the modern man and a mate who retains the incalculable impulses of a more elemental nature. Hardy's statement of these situations is all the more instructive by virtue of his concentration on this primitive feature of human character. In old days Hardy's vision of the primitive and elemental, as manifested in women, was resented by many; feminists were wont to compare Hardy's women, to their disadvantage, with Meredith's. From the ethical standpoint that preference for Meredith's women was then justifiable. To-day, perhaps, when we no longer need to rebel against Victorianism, and are able with him " to see beauty in ugliness," we may view the psychological traits of Hardy's women without prejudice, and even recognise in them an element of permanent veracity.

HAVELOCK ELLIS.

FOREWORD TO THE ENGLISH TRANSLATION

BEFORE allowing this book to set forth upon a new mission we feel that, if to-day it is to travel beyond the point at which it aimed yesterday, a special prologue is necessary. We do not presume to introduce English readers to him whom Edmond Jaloux has impressively styled the "Homer of British pessimism." This is merely the testimony of a Frenchman regarding his work. It is in particular a proof of the interest aroused in us by all the forms of thought and sensibility that we meet with in the realm of English intellectual life. Contact through the interpretation of a writer of genius with a civilization which, however near it may be to our own, is none the less entirely distinct from it, is always moving and possesses the same attractive force as the great open spaces. All prose and poetry that reach us through the medium of some language other than our own liberate within us fresh or atavistic emotions and nothing is more " bracing," as you would say, for the mind than that air which one breathes when one strives to break in upon an alien consciousness. Once outside the scale of national literature we become aware of other notes, other tones and other modulations, which we wish to hear, because they correspond with a kind of expectation and desire already present within us.

French criticism has always bestowed attention

upon Hardy. A glance at the final pages of this book
will make that amply clear.[1] A proof of an admirable
alertness appears in an article in the *Revue des Deux
Mondes* of 15th December, 1875, which seems to have
opened the lists. Under the title *Le Roman Pastoral
en Angleterre* Léon Boucher published an instructed
and sympathetic study of *Under the Greenwood Tree,
A Pair of Blue Eyes*, and *Far From the Madding
Crowd*. After a proper appreciation of Hardy's
dubious beginning with *Desperate Remedies*, the
critic draws an unexpected and profoundly sugges-
tive parallel between Boileau's *Lutrin* and *Under the
Greenwood Tree*, for the subject of both books is
essentially the same. He makes, however, a detailed
and comprehensive analysis of *Far From the Madding
Crowd*, showing that he has observed and appreciated
its arresting qualities.

The *Tribute* prepared by Charles du Bos and
published by the *Revue Nouvelle* in February, 1928,
was addressed to the living Hardy. At the moment
when all the contributions had been brought together,
Hardy or the handful of ashes which remained of
him had already been laid at Westminster, to an
immortal exile, far from Wessex, itself rendered
immortal. It was perhaps of little moment, for
Hardy already knew what a tribute of gratitude was
on its way to him and thus had a kind of foretaste of
it. For it was a new promise of the fruits to be reaped
from his labour.

This gesture, with which we ourselves had the
honour to be associated, included tributes from men
of such distinction as René Boylesve, already dead,
who had specially written the pages which he signed,

1 See the Bibliography pp. 212-19.

from Charles du Bos, from G. d'Hargest, from
Franz Hellens, from Edmond Jaloux, from Ramon
Fernandez, from Jean Schlumberger, and from J. L.
Vaudoyer, and from English writers such as James
Joyce, John Middleton Murray, Eden Phillpotts, and
an extract from *de Temps Retrouvé*, wherein Marcel
Proust paid his homage as an æsthete to the English
artist.

The mere fact that such a tribute associating some
celebrated and even illustrious names should have
appeared in a review still in its youth, in one of those
reviews which are reputed to give a rough outline
of the literature of to-morrow, shows how large and
attentive audience Hardy found among us, particularly among those writers who are still in the fray.

In the invaluable documents constituted by the
correspondence (1905-1914) of those two young
writers prematurely carried off, Alain Fournier and
Jacques Rivière, the name of Hardy occurs very
often, side by side with those of Barrès, Claudel and
Gide, who were their masters. After reading *Tess*,
the future, rarely gifted author of *Le Grand Meaulnes*,
wrote to the future author of *Aimée* : " The course
of my ideas have been somewhat changed." The
position occupied by Hardy in this exchange of
letters is an indication of his influence.

On the day following Hardy's death an impressive
unanimity manifested itself during a brief moment,
given up to the contemplation of his work. French
newspapers and reviews piously saluted the dead
writer.

Is there in the genius of Thomas Hardy some
element of kinship with the genius of our race?
What has the land of Descartes to offer to those

who would understand and comment upon Hardy?
Is not this, perhaps, the real truth, that in spite of
the insularity of his temperament Hardy is very
little insular, is indeed continental and, therefore,
nearer to us? Further on we shall discuss everything that attaches him to a chapter of our own
literary history, still present in the minds of all, the
chapter of Naturalism.

In any case, Hardy did not manifest any dis-
pleasure at the tributes of sympathy extended to him
from France. That this is so is clear from the preface
which he wrote for a French translation of the *The
Dynasts*, reproduced in the special number of the
Revue Nouvelle. We ourselves heard him expound
in favourable terms the hypothesis of a distant connection with Alexander Hardy, the writer of tragedies
of the Hotel de Bourgogne. And that proves that
he was not ashamed of his ancestors from Jersey.

In your language there is a mysterious word,
full of poetry and for us almost untranslatable,
"glamour." Of such sort is the charm which his
work irradiates so freely, and which keeps us per-
petually in a state of fervent enthusiasm. It is for
this reason that the Hardyan cycle has diligent ad-
mirers among us, grateful for this initiation by the
medium of local themes into the grand and harsh
modulations of rural life, into their application to
the central problems of destiny and of the species.

The Human Pair in the Work of Thomas Hardy;
the title of this volume itself shows from what point
of view we have considered the work, without in any
way wishing to derogate from its other aspects.
Hardy showed neither surprise nor anxiety regarding this enquiry and the designation attached to it.

The English formula under which we presented it to him, the formula which you have here, inspired him with no alarm. It accorded too intimately with our convictions, it was too much in harmony with our scheme of work to admit of any modification in response to subsequent manifestations of surprise.

Thomas Hardy remains an august example for us. For us, Dorchester and Max Gate are two spots, human no less than literary, two stations where the traveller may pause to meditate upon the creations of the sensibility, testing them as it were by a touchstone upon the very flints of which the village roads are formed. At Dorchester the legend of Hardy was a living legend, local and discreet. In the windows of the small stationers the collections of post-cards told of Stonehenge or of the famous tower in *Far From the Madding Crowd*. At the hotel we were treated with more consideration when it was discovered that we had been received at Max Gate and that we were going back there.

Hardy lived a life of seclusion. Every morning he went for a walk in the country, attentively scanning the changes that the years bring even to the fields. He also saw a few friends. Mrs Florence Hardy surrounded the poet with that warm zone of silence which did not exclude the powerful vibrations of Wessex. The man who once had taken part in the literary life of London had shut fast his door. He lived almost outside his time.

He had just received a letter from Dreiser, and the American novelist asked permission to call upon the old man. The latter, on the defensive and always timid, fearing perhaps the dubious kind of publicity that he might receive from a Transatlantic interviewer, seemed little disposed to receive the author of *An American Tragedy*. Hardy was clearly no longer in touch with the latest events in the world of literature, and Dreiser's youthful glory conveyed nothing to the aloof and cautious deity.

I spoke on behalf of the request. I thought that I had converted Hardy to the point of admitting the legitimacy of the visit. But perhaps I shall never know whether that sovereign, so little eager for tribute, received Theodore Dreiser.

Further on you will read the story of the time which I passed at Max Gate. It seemed as if the sage had bidden farewell to his glory, even to his work and to that long patience which constitutes genius. What a surprise to find the architect of that rough masonry so puny, a being almost apart, it seemed, from what he had constructed.

If, in his presence, I showed interest in some knick-knack which recalled one of his own works, he would say with detachment: " I don't care for old curiosities."

Do not such words as these show how much more pre-occupied Hardy was with human interests, and that in his eyes the fundamental question of the pair and of destiny was of far greater importance than mullioned windows, notes on local colour or accessories derived from the past? Such an answer could justly be received as a commentary. It showed that there existed a profound agreement between our enterprise and the writer's own vision of his work.

On the way back from Hardy's House we entered one of those square-towered Anglican churches, surrounded by tombstones which in their modesty and antiquity present death in a humbler and more

familiar light.   It was about seven o'clock in the
evening and we expected to find ourselves in an
empty temple.   We only found an old woman busy
in the sacristy.   She led us towards the choir.   She
was a naive, worthy creature.   " Our vicar is away
in your country for the Fêtes of Falaise in Caen.   He
is a descendant of one of the companions of William
the Conqueror.   We've a beautiful church.   Come
and see it."   She then took us to the vestry to show
us the red vestments and lace of the choir boys.   Was
not red her favourite colour with its promise of pomp
and ceremony ?

" You can come to the service to-morrow morning.
It is in this church that you will see the most beautiful things.   It is almost like a Catholic mass."

Later, when I recalled these memories, it seemed
to me to be a thing characteristic of the race that
Hardy, whose work rose like a pagan protest against
all theology, should have come to rest in a sanctuary
where his remains were received with full ceremonial
by the clergy and the principal dignitaries of the
State.   It was as if the memorial stone of Westminster
had covered with its own shadow that hostility to
religion, and sanctified it as that of a great voice
which must not be allowed to die away.

And suddenly I heard again within myself the
peasant accents of the old woman in the church and,
finding in them that same note of frank sincerity and
hospitable simplicity, I was fain to think of other
rustics, of those of Shakespeare and Molière, living
avowals of so much that is essential, types whose
genuineness no one has ever been able to dispute.

July 1929.

CHAPTER I

INTRODUCTION

WHAT has this book to offer? It is a monograph, devoted to a single aspect of Hardy's work, a contribution to the study of a problem in philosophy and the art of literature. Thus conceived, these pages could find no room for any eccentric developments regarding the character either of the novels or of the poems. Our essay is, accordingly, addressed to initiated readers.

In dealing with so vast a work, it seemed legitimate to accord a special consideration to two or three fundamental questions which share between them the interest aroused by the work as a whole. Examined exhaustively and in isolation, they gain by being compared with the metamorphoses which they are made to undergo in other works and by other temperaments.

It thus becomes our task, after the general survey which must precede any enquiry, to probe deeply into a text, calmly to hollow out its galleries, and to bear away from this work of prospecting a dossier upon which the final discussion may be based.

The writer set out with no pre-conceived plan, no exact regard for order and equilibrium in his efforts to group and to connect the observations derived

1

from the *Wessex Novels*, *Wessex Tales*, and *Wessex Poems*. The whole received form and arrangement from the scrutiny and comparison of the notes.

Several chapters merely describe the evolution of the drama of the sexes. The same causes are repeatedly chosen as starting-points for reaching the same results, in order to verify and throw light upon numerous facts of a psychological and even of a physiological character.

At times no doubt there may occur something analogous to what is known in physics as a phenomenon of interference, a disadvantage possibly prejudicial to the effectiveness of a pure dissertation. But in this place it is our duty to cover the full extent of a concept and to fix its limits with the utmost exactness.

Hardy held loyally to certain ideas with a grim faith. Without always assigning to them the same position, but with the same intensity of expression, he pursued them throughout variants resembling one another like the varieties of the same species in natural history. This study is therefore less inspired by the chronological order of the novels or poems and their individual characteristics than by the unities of ideas and definite tendencies revealing themselves therein. We have striven to penetrate to the essential matter, at times even to the abstract physiognomy, while ignoring the incidental and gratuitous character of certain aspects.

Always partial in its foregone conclusions, Hardy's work leaves indelible imprints, outlining the convergence of the furrows hollowed out and of the main laws governing their general direction.

In a natural spirit of mimicry the critic is tempted

to reconstruct upon his own plan by a similar kind of procedure the creative process, the secrets of which he has sought to lay bare, the inmost life of which he would search out and expound.

In 1895 Hardy considered his work as a novelist completed. He could think, not without reason, that he had said all that he had to say, and that *Tess of the d'Urbervilles* and *Jude the Obscure* gave to his prose-work its conclusion and crown. The poet did not disappear at the same time as the novelist. He survived, or, to be more exact, was resuscitated. One may say that until the hour when, a few weeks before his death, he was stricken down by that bronchitis which was to carry him off, the patriarch of Max Gate never completely abandoned writing, and the poems of his last years mounted in a solitary apotheosis of old age, serene and almost cheerful. Indeed, Hardy even affected to regard his poems as his most durable monument. The master himself wrote to us in these terms shortly after the appearance of an article[1] devoted to him. One may bend without fear over a work so nobly sculptured. For if they have spread their patina upon it, the years have none the less left its reliefs unimpaired. The very disappearance of Thomas Hardy now gives us the needed perspective.

The various collections of stories and the fourteen novels which appeared between 1871 and 1895, throwing upon the affairs of the heart sometimes a harsh, often a savage light, put us in possession of Hardy's ideas regarding the human pair. The volumes of verse, which followed, offering in epitome swift-moving scenes and more tersely expressed thoughts,

[1] *La Revue Nouvelle*, April 1927.

in no way invalidated the message of the prose-writer.

If the ensuing excellence of the thinker and artist is heralded in the first novels, it would certainly seem that the whole cycle prepared the way for the two last[1]. These resemble a pediment, crowning the completed work of a temple.

The whole work gives the impression of an effort directed towards an end. A creation inspired by the will, it asserts its dogmas and advances its evidence. Throughout the work of Balzac the passion for money proclaims itself to be the dominant force of society. Hardy, who sees in love at once the creative and motor force, accords it first place among human preoccupations.[2] To the artist who bathes every day in a stream of landscapes, Nature remains something very near and very animal, and in such a setting love remains the essential function. Upon these uplands and moors or amid these valleys the human couple is only active in pursuit of the tasks which have devolved upon the artisans of life. According to the poet's admission love, notwithstanding the uneasy slavery and mortification which he depicts at every moment, none the less remains the great motive force of existence.

> " But—after love what comes?
>   A scene that lours,
>   A few sad vacant hours,
>   And then the curtain."[3]

It is thus legitimate to devote the whole of these

1 *Tess of the d'Urbervilles* and *Jude the Obscure*.
2 " . . . . strongest passion known to humanity "—*Jude the Obscure* (Preface).
3 *Time's Laughingstocks.*

pages solely to the human pair. How narrowly this study is limited was made clear at the outset. And yet when brought within its true proportions this book approaches an important problem of literature, of philosophy, perhaps even of morality. It treats of one of those eternal themes which the pens of novelists or poets will never succeed in exhausting. Within such a work as that of Hardy the question of the union of the sexes assumes infinite dimensions and thus has its place in the movement of thought in the latter part of the nineteenth century. Not to grasp the full significance of this would be to misunderstand one of the essential aspects of this writer's works.

At once an analysis and a synthesis, this book seeks to point out the manifold correspondences, the innumerable echoes, the answers from afar and the possible prolongations, suggested by a work of this stature. Herein are revealed, immoveable and tenacious amid their variety, the permanent laws of the mind and of the feelings.

To carry out this task, criticism cannot remain purely æsthetic and academic. It must become also historical and philosophical. For to give these works their full dynamic force, their position in and their relations with the universe must be marked out and defined. The dispute over subject and object can only be settled by this collaboration between methods too often opposed or made the subject of empty distinctions. We hear it stated that the work should in itself suffice, that it needs no commentary. That is to some extent true. But if the object has a beauty proper to itself, that beauty becomes real only by and in the subject. Who, then, is there that will educate

his sensibility and his judgment? Therein lies a
mission of fundamental importance. Purely æsthetic
criticism tends to advance upon the work without
deriving any special guidance from those avenues and
paths which lead towards it along the lines of the
historical method. Philosophical criticism not only
examines the work in itself; it tries to discover the
relations between the mode of expression and the
thing expressed. It tries to surprise the secrets of
the artist who, amid the flux of all things, desired to
revive in its full sequence a period of life, to restore
it or to transpose it in all its plasticity, its colours
and its rhythm with the aid of words long worn out.
Hypothesis or intuition will sometimes allow us to
rediscover the path leading to the living synthesis
realised by the artist, who at the outset was only
equipped with a mere handful of facts and impressions, gathered up in the course of his experience.
When it is possible to reconstruct this labour one
penetrates to the very depths of a work, to its
genesis; one beholds it emerging from the laboratory
of the spirit. In the interests of a knowledge at once
ampler, more human and more real, one follows the
processes of the thought along zig-zag routes, the
" why " of which is hidden from the creator himself.

Literary criticism, in fact, knows no absolute,
unique, exclusive, perfect, and above all truly
scientific method. Alike, whether it appeals to
Sainte-Beuve, to Taine, to Angellier, to Rémy de
Gourmont or to M. Gustave Lanson, each conception
has its own share of the truth, its special advantages.
Different methods of approach may be advocated,
but in the final analysis everything comes back to
the reaction of a temperament in the presence of a

work. If there are facts before which one must bow under penalty of failure, no good result can emerge without that sensibility upon which all fine judgment depends.

For a critic worthy the name the attitude adopted by a writer towards life should not be a ground for any condemnation in principle. Why, like M. Eugène Montfort,[1] reproach Hardy with his pessimism in the name of some sort of dogma, if indeed dogma there be in such matters? Is pessimism a blemish like poverty of imagination or a restricted vocabulary? Neither eulogy, nor reserve, neither blame, nor perhaps regret: there is no question of any such things, where pessimism is the issue. A sentiment which rises to such a degree of implacability and to so rich a profusion is surely not without grandeur. Marginal reflections can only express surprise and disorientation. An author may think what he will of life, judge it to be absurd or exalt it; it is not in virtue of that that his book is a success or a failure. The merit of the work may be distinct from the theories which he believes himself to hold and does not prevent them from being detestable.

Let us pass our verdict upon the quality of this pessimism, enumerate its weaknesses, its lacunæ, and its contradictions. Let us, if it be possible, adopt the role of experts upon its quality. But let us leave the writer his freedom of choice.

To write " I prefer Wordsworth's optimism to Hardy's pessimism " is, once more, to give utterance to a sufficiently sterile preference. The thing must be judged on its own merits, in the light of com-

[1] Eugène Montfort, *Les Marges*, 1903-1908. (Bibliothèque des Marges, 1913).

parisons too, but of comparisons borrowed from spheres near at hand. There would be no sense in preferring Chartres to the Propylæum. The two forms of architecture are separate in time and place; no useful purpose is served in opposing them to one another. No code of values can be extracted from personal taste.

To refuse Dostojevsky his place among his peers on the ground that he did not choose his heroes from good society is equivalent to wishing to impose an ideal which should deprive the temperament of its rightful liberties on an arbitrary pretext.

A Wessex plant, nourished on the sap of Wessex, Hardy's work raises all the problems. Wandering near Dorchester, amid the damp meadows leading to Talbothays, and meeting those peasant-women who render service about the august rites of the dairy, in their black hats, recalling the straw hats worn by the women of Provence in the Saracen Highlands,[1] one would fain conjure forth from their common shell the entrancing figure of Tess. Is it not an effect of that special charm, of the gift of transmutation that in *The Mayor of Casterbridge* one sees the legionaries of Hadrian starting to life on the worn-out steps of the amphitheatre? By the extent of the gulf between anonymous, indifferent reality and the work which emerges from the writer's transfiguring hand, we may measure the power of his genius, the amplitude of his capacity.

Hardy's work has attracted criticism by its seductive charm; it has also appealed to it in virtue of its depth. In addition to the general studies devoted to the work and to the man, to the artist and to the

[1] Les Maures.

thinker, more limited studies have appeared like the
book of Mr H. B. Grimsditch on *Character and Environment in the Novels of Thomas Hardy*, that of
Mr J. W. Beach, *The Technique of Thomas Hardy*,
and many others.

Coming back to general studies the volume of Mr
Hedgcock (1911) comprises a complete, judicious and
methodical work, which confers the greatest honour
upon English criticism.   Written as a thesis for the
Doctorship of Letters at the Sorbonne, this work was
composed in French, while the general scheme was
inspired by our University methods.   There was at
one time a question of translating it into English, a
task which Mr Hedgcock could easily have undertaken in view of his nationality.   But Hardy, who
rose in energetic protest against certain of the inter-
pretations, was definitely unfavourable to the project,
as he himself narrated to me.   Fault has been found
with Mr Hedgcock—certainly unjustly—on the score
of long summaries of the novels which are, however,
so useful to the student or to the seeker eager to
explore the Hardyan cycle more rapidly.   This book
may undoubtedly be compared with the most highly
appreciated studies coming from the other side of
the Channel, with the more distant work of Lionel
Johnson[1] and the nearer pages of Lascelles Abercrombie.[2]

And yet the whole of this critical literature seems
to have neglected two problems.   On the one hand the
very evident connection between the philosophical
realism of Hardy, the novelist, and the purely
naturalistic movement, on the other hand, the rela-

1 *The Art of Thomas Hardy* (1894).
2 *Thomas Hardy.   A critical study* (1912).

tions between that writer's metaphysics and the governing ideas of his age.

Upon the sources of Hardy's thought, as they may be discovered if one retraces these two streams of influence, all has not been said, even in Mr Brennecke's book on Hardy and Schopenhauer (*Hardy's Universe*). We have found gaps which we have striven to fill to the extent interesting to our researches.

CHAPTER II

HARDY'S POSITION IN THE MOVEMENT OF ENGLISH
REALISM AND NATURALISM

ENGLISH LITERATURE AND SEX

" There is no such thing as a moral or an immoral
book."

OSCAR WILDE.

" Man alone is imperfect. To be happy he must
find a mate."

PASCAL.

IN its most rugged pages Hardy's work contains
a vigorous study of the human pair. This study,
at once solid and sombre, has all the character of
a demonstration. As treated by our author it even
assumes the marks of necessity.

The two beings destined to love each other form
the two halves of one and the same thing, two mole-
cules of a single body. Nature designed them to re-
unite in a perfect whole.[1] One is tempted to recall
the merciless phrase employed by Joyce in *Ulysses*:
" They clasped and sundered, did the Coupler's
Will."

What is the source of this driving impulse to make

1 " The two halves intended to form a perfect whole." *A Few
Crusted Characters*. " The two halves of an approximately perfect
whole. . . ." *Tess of the d'Urbervilles*. " Since the first two
sighing half-hearts made a whole." (*News for the Mother*). *Time's
Laughingstocks*.

the best possible match between a man and a woman ?
It springs from physiological necessity. Either the
two beings are nothing without one another, or they
remain two mere isolated individuals without that
union which perpetuates the species. This, the most
inward of emotions, unconsciously impresses such a
woman as Eustacia with the feeling that she has
found her most perfect complement in a man.[1]
Hardy possesses the gift of discovering in every pair
the elementary nucleus, the two creatures clasped
together, as at the creation of the world. " The
spectral half-compounded, aqueous light, which pervaded the open mead, impressed them with a feeling
of isolation, as if they were Adam and Eve."[2] To
adopt the admirable expression of M. Charles Du
Bos,[3] in the story of every idyll, " we always find
the infancy of the world." At the foundation of this
vast epic of the flesh this element invariably appears,
and the eternal innocence of the world expresses itself
by the ever new and primitive awakening to love of
beings faithful to the stock from which they are
sprung.

As conceived by Hardy, in its most absolute and
most brutal significance, the human pair emerges
with special clearness in the great diptych formed by
the stories of Tess and Jude. In *Tess of the
d'Urbervilles* Alexander and Angel successively express two irreducible types of man gravitating about
the same woman, and the pair appears and reappears, each time transfigured and invested with a

---

[1] " . . . . her perfect complement in attainments, appearance
and age ". *The Return of the Native.*
[2] *Tess of the d'Urbervilles.* Chap. XX, p. 169.
[3] Quelques traits du visage de Thomas Hardy. Charles Du Bos.
La Revue Nouvelle. February 1928.

new value. In *Jude the Obscure* Arabella and Sue,
those two opposite poles of femininity, awaken, each
in her own turn, in the breast of an unfinished, or
better expressed, of an incomplete male character
the echoes of a sensuality, still bearing the imprints
of rusticity and of the intellectualism of a primitive
type. To complete this general view and to set forth
the full measure of harmful elements contained in
each example, it might be said that Alexander and
Angel are for different reasons, and each on his own
account, the authors of the mischief that overtakes
Tess, just as Arabella and Sue merely relieve one
another in the process of destroying Jude.

In each of these two cases, as almost always with
Hardy, the passions aroused by love are examined
in a setting deliberately chosen for its proximity to
Nature and thus find conditions which assure them
all the unity of a primordial, elemental sentiment,
stripped of the varnish of politeness and convention.

Other pictures of the pair appear throughout all the
books, where the problem of the sexes is raised. In
Far From the Madding Crowd it is a single woman
whose charm rivets the attention of three men; it is
the story of three loves, reflected in the same feminine
mirror. *The Return of the Native* deals with the fate
of two couples between whom moves the ruddy form
of the shrewd Diggory Venn, the good genius of the
heath.

The writer knows how to ignore such useless em-
bellishments as the tricks of sentimentality. He
retains only the essence of the emotion which he
describes. We would often compare the Olympian
author of the *Wessex Novels* with the Tolstoy of the
Kreutzer Sonata for the truthful spirit in which he

has specifically treated the difficult problem of the relations between the sexes. But Tolstoy mounts to the assault of the conjugal stronghold, whereas Hardy only exercises the right of subjecting it to a pitiless scrutiny. On the other hand the freedom of the English novelist penetrates to depths which Zola's audacity never reached, even when with the glance of a practising doctor the master of Médan probes the relations between man and woman.[1] And the reason for that is that Hardy concentrated upon this capital point of human destiny the whole effort of a truly creative power of observation, thereby rising to views consistent with a complete system of thought.

If the fundamental elements of this study are contained in the two masterpieces, which we have mentioned, the other novels must not be neglected. They are, no doubt, less complete in their significance for the point of view with which we are concerned, but we must search in them for preparatory or complementary data. Like flying buttresses in a cathedral they will group themselves about the same nave.

Hardy's first novels yield us principally impressions, already definite in their tendency, but devoid of system. With " Tess " and " Jude " a real discussion of ideas is set on foot and the author's philosophy is defined. Or rather it is perhaps that his two heroes, brothers in misfortune, are exposed to such iniquities proceeding from destiny, from con-

---

[1] Zola writes in the second preface to *Thérèse Raquin* (1868): " I chose as my characters. . . . individuals lured on to every action of their lives by the fatality of the flesh. . . . The loves of my two heroes are the satisfaction of a need; the murder which they commit is a consequence of their adultery. . . . In a word, I have only one desire : given a sturdy man and an unsatisfied woman. . . to hurl them into a violent drama." (pp. II and III, Edition Charpentier, 1893.)

vention, and from the character of man, that the
claims and protests of the human pair wounded and
piteous seem to rise from the mournful sympathy of
the author.

The freedom with which Hardy treated this serious
problem had its due part in provoking scandal.
Deliberately arraying itself in a veil of gauze, English literature but rarely contemplated love, save
under the chaste adornment of its insular conventions. The English novel did not, in fact, remain
faithful to the tradition of the novelists and story-
tellers of the eighteenth century, such as De Foe,
Fielding, Sterne and Smollett, in whom there came to
life again as in Hogarth the whole gallantry of an
epoch. Under the influence of Sir Walter Scott and
of his medieval romanticism the fashion of unreality
became good form, and people steered clear of anything like an acceptance of life. Throughout the
whole of Scott's works the sound of a kiss is hardly
ever heard. This deliberate bias often narrowed the
horizon of the great writers throughout a reign of
sixty-three years, which carried the power of Britain
to its zenith. Victoria ruled from 1837 to 1901, and
it was during this reign—the longest ever known in
England—that a poet could write :

> " God's in his heaven,
>   All is right with the world."

But the pomp of majesty sought isolation in a
virtuous rusticity. In the face of such an august
example the century adapted itself to a measure of
ugliness.

Crises in domestic politics or difficulties with the
colonies could never call in question this optimism,

which sprang from the process of growth itself. Even
science seemed for a long time to labour in the interests of order and well-being. Notwithstanding the
dissent expressed in such resonant tones by Carlyle
and Ruskin, Newman and Kingsley, an era of content,
originating in industrial prosperity surpassing anything previously known, separated the middle classes
from all that could disturb their felicity or challenge
their good name. In their satirical works writers
must touch only upon the superficial aspects of
society. In that respect Thackeray is of all the most
representative. In the preface to *Pendennis* he shews
the full extent of the reserve to which the novelist
must submit.

The Reform Bill of 1832 had already deprived the
territorial aristocracy of its political influence in the
interests of a middle class, favoured by the advance
of industry. In course of time the very accumula-
tion of wealth which raised a section of the middle
classes to the heights of prosperity was to divide
the whole class into two distinct parts, the contented
on the one side, the embittered on the other. It
is the latter who will be attracted by the materialistic interpretation of history, that instrument of
propaganda, employed by the Trade Unions and the
Fabians to stampede the camp of prejudice.

How massive, then, was the stone which a Hardy
and other writers, George Gissing, George Moore,
Whiteing, Arthur Morrison, Hubert Crackanthorpe,
Lucas Malet, George Egerton flung with a grim
agility into the stagnant pool of Puritanism.

How many virtuous women-readers must have
cried out in protest when they studied the sensual
picture of an Arabella. Lord Tennyson himself, the

poet-laureate, came forward as the semi-official pro-
tagonist of idyllic morality in *Locksley Hall, Sixty
Years After* (1886). He sounds the alarm against
the champions of the new school, charging them with
corrupting the treasures of innocence and purity by
contact with their own filthiness. As late as 1894, in
the first number of so emancipated a publication as
the *Yellow Book*, a study by Arthur Waugh,
" Reticence in Literature," attacks the development
of Realism, reproaching certain writers with out-
raging motherhood by depicting the processes of
birth. But in Hardy's hands Victorian sentimentalism, already bitterly criticised by Meredith,
crumbles under the weight of terrible truths. The
injustice, the hypocrisy and the vanity of the structure are pitilessly denounced in disregard of all
established admirations, be they sincere or interested. Moreover with that biting pen the very
audacity of the picture undoubtedly becomes one of
the great characteristics of the work itself. As we
look back along the years, it appears in part in the
guise of a document produced with a special view
to the indictment of Victorianism.

When upon the background of the stellar universe[1]
a Hardy cuts out as upon a screen the infinitely small
and yet so complex silhouette of the human pair and
opposes it in a manner, at times recalling Pascal, to
the agonizing serenity of infinite space, it really
seems as if the whole romance were palpitating in the
hearts of two poor beings compounded of flesh. The
author demonstrates to us that it is only love and its
realisation ever hedged about by difficulty that is of
importance here, even if our thoughts, like those of

[1] *Two on a Tower.*

Saint-Cleeve, are exclusively occupied in following
the celestial revolutions on high, which reflect their
course in the pupils of his eyes in wondrous nails of
gold, sewn upon the velvet mantle of nights of love.
A representation of the infinitely little side by side
with the infinitely great : the sidereal immensity
covering with its starry tent the microcosm of passion.

We have recourse to this example to illustrate more
fully the weight borne by the pair in the most
" crucial " parts of Hardy's books, and to show
how the whole equipment of a novel, its whole procession of accessory characters,[1] its evocations of
places and landscapes have only been created and
worked up, in order to throw a stronger light upon a
twofold central figure. The human pair thus becomes
the fragile association upon which rests the fate
meted out to humanity. For such a study to have
been possible at all, and for it to have appeared in
its due season, the course had first to be outlined
or the track at least indicated.

Certain curves of the route had already been
clearly suggested by Charles Reade and Wilkie
Collins, and Hardy was not the first to venture upon
it. Charles Reade (1814-1884), a realist by temperament, was prior to Zola in his use of the documentary method. Wilkie Collins (1824-1889) was at once
a realist and an imaginative writer. His realism
resting upon a documentary basis preceded and made
possible other efforts in the direction of sincerity

---

1 " Unessential in many cases to the conduct of the mere
narrative, they and the landscapes around them yet serve to
emphasise the force of that narrative : far from being picturesque
accessories, they form the chorus whose office is to insist upon
the stable moralities, the tried wisdom and experience, with which
the fortunes of the chief actors are in contrast ". Lionel Johnson
The Art of Thomas Hardy, 1894.

and frankness. The coming of realism in England had already been prepared for by the analytical methods and the psychological penetration of which Browning and George Eliot had supplied excellent patterns. But this will to frankness, at times even to crudity, did not readily show itself on the other side of the Channel. There it seemed as if literature desired to live swaddled in the folds of its own tendencies, insular and even provincial. In 1865 Matthew Arnold proclaimed in his *Essays in Criticism* the necessity for criticism to become European. In taking this step he was betraying a significant need, the need to denounce Cant and the Philistinism against which a Byron had shattered himself to pieces. The drama of a revision of all ethical views was about to unfold itself. The discoveries and impatience of a new world were about to assail the bourgeois and Philistine spirit of a society slumbering amid its ease and its prejudices. Sexual questions were to be approached without prudery, without affectation, and if possible without reticence. The framework of " respectability " so congenial to a Thackeray was to be shattered. Herein the example reeived from France was to be infectious and decisive. Flaubert, Zola, the brothers Goncourt, and Maupassant had been, each for a different reason, the apostles of a new religion in art which would shed its rays far and wide in England.

In the final analysis Realism and Naturalism only express two aspects or two degrees of one and the same thing, of the same attitude towards the facts of life. The masters of those schools did not conceive themselves to be under any obligation to proscribe anything in literature that might shock or displease. They placed themselves above prejudice. To mention two dates is enough to give a general indication of the development of the English novel during the period when it was influenced by this school of writers or was imitating them. *The Return of the Native* dates from 1878; *Thérèse Raquin* appeared in 1867. These two epoch-making books were published at an interval of eleven years, and however debatable such chronological frontiers may be, the space of from ten to twelve years may thus be said to mark the distance covered by the English novel in reaching, at least to some extent, the point at which ours had arrived. But, therefore, for the early successes achieved in England by the French books, Hardy would never have been granted licence to give expression to his temperament. There were many writers who maintained the closest relations with France, from Charles Reade, who adapted Zola for the stage, down to Hubert Crackanthorpe, the disciple of Maupassant, the suicide of the Seine, to say nothing of George Moore, who acquired the freedom of Paris, Richard Whiteing, whose literary career began with books on Paris, George Gissing who, when quite young, learned to speak French with a Provençal accent, and died in the Pyrenees tended by a French woman, who had become the companion of his life, and George du Maurier, whose sham Parisianism did not rob " Trilby " of its vogue. A writer and a draughtsman, du Maurier illustrated the first edition of *The Hand of Ethelberta*.[1]

[1] Hardy always denied ever having yielded to the influence of any school of writers. Let us bear this statement in mind. Yet, like all those who emulated him, for the sake of the audacity of the subjects selected, Hardy read French. In 1887 the novelist went on a long journey through Europe, visiting in particular parts of Italy and Switzerland. Coming at such a time to the Continent, he could not altogether have escaped the influences of the

In our country *Madame Bovary* gave the signal for great frankness in depicting manners and customs in the provinces and the ravages inflicted by sentimentality upon the heart of a middle-class woman. English writers could, therefore, go back further than Zola to find suitable models in French literature. Emma Bovary was to hear a surprising answering call in Eustacia Vye in *The Return of the Native*, that other victim of disillusionment.   As Zola expressed it in a study entitled *Le Naturalisme au Theatre*, in writing *Madame Bovary* Flaubert " aimed at shewing that one could treat of the provincial lower middle classes with the fullness and the power put forth by Homer, when speaking of Greek heroes."[1]

The Return of the Native (1878) also reaches the emotional level of some antique episode where the voices of destiny are heard muttering, and where the forces of the environment are banded together. Later, in the first chapter of *The Woodlanders* (1887), Hardy was to write in so many words that dramas of a Sophoclean power sometimes take place in the villages of Wessex.[2]   Thus he puts upon the lives of the peasants a robe of tragic dignity and the concep-

Naturalism then prevalent.   We must not be misled by such denials as have emanated from Hardy in regard to other points. Hardy studied French when quite young.   Later he followed courses in French at King's College, London.   He travelled several times in France and often stayed in Paris.   If he never acquired a perfect knowledge of our language, it is difficult to suppose that he could have remained entirely outside French influence, particularly living his life in London society, where he met so many literary people.

1 *Le Roman Expérimental* (a study of Naturalism in the Theatre, p. 119).   Bibl. Charpentier, 1888.

2 " It was one of those sequestered spots outside the gates of the world . . . yet where, from time to time, dramas of a grandeur and unity truly Sophoclean are enacted in the real, by virtue of concentrated passions and closely knit interdependence of the lives therein."   *The Woodlanders*, p. 5.

tion, which Zola discovered in Flaubert and which
the author of *La Terre* was himself to seize upon, is
once more taken up and extended. In *The Return
of the Native* Eustacia Vye, whom Hardy makes a
Queen of the Night, might rank with Jocasta, with
Hecuba, with Polyxena and with other unhappy
women. In these pages the author offers no painting
designed to trick the eye; he flings aside all outworn
devices. Thus a true relationship exists between two
such novels as *The Return of the Native* and *Madame
Bovary*. Candour and loftiness of tone make them
two works of the same style.

The last lines of *Madame Bovary*, as traced by
Flaubert, bring no element of consolation. On the
contrary, Charles Bovary dies, leaving his daughter
in poverty, and the only victor is the chemist Homais,
who receives the Legion of Honour. It is the picture
of the incurable wretchedness of a probably doomed
humanity, portraying the nothingness, whereof man
is compounded, even prior to the coming of death.
From such volumes there streams forth an intense
and bitter emotion of sadness. This sadness is not
absent from the works of the brothers Goncourt and
of Maupassant. These writers choose as their types
beings whose gestures and desires were determined
in advance and whose motives might be compared to
straws swept along by the currents of Nature. Their
numerous books, in which the questions of conjugal
incompatibility and of free love play so large a role,
were to find a considerable public in Great Britain.
Again French fiction revived technique in England
by opposing unity of plan and action to diffuse and
intricate intrigues. The taste for French literature
was to re-awaken with greater vividness. It was

only towards the year 1883, that is after the appearance of Hardy's first novels, that the translations of
Zola, of Alphonse Daudet, and some years later of
the brothers Goncourt, of Flaubert and of Maupassant, began to circulate in England. These works
did not fail to encounter a vigorous opposition on the
part of the critics. A section of opinion constantly
reproached these writers with finding satisfaction in
the foul and with sapping the moral foundations of
society. There was, too, an element of risk in the
struggle. The whole question actually reached the
House of Commons, and was shortly after decided at
Bow Street Police Court. Already seventy years of
age, the publisher, Henry Vizetelly, was brought
before the Central Criminal Court in 1889. The
penalty for his boldness in publishing translations of
Zola was three months' imprisonment. One hundred
and fifty writers, statesmen, scholars and artists,
among whom one notes Hardy's name, attached their
signatures to a petition. It was the protest of
intelligence.

Thus, after centuries of Protestantism, the country
of dramatists such as Shakespeare and Ben Jonson,
whose genius has never been surpassed in energy and
outspokenness, could still not tolerate the mention in
a book of the birth of a natural child or the adventures of an adulteress. Or, at least, these subjects
could not be approached without circumlocution.
These years 1890-91 and 1892 undoubtedly marked
the culminating point of the struggle. In 1890 there
appeared in England the translation of Zola's *Roman
Expérimental*, published in Paris in 1880, but at the
same time the ultra-conservative *Quarterly Review*
printed articles in which the French Realistic and

Naturalistic movement was denounced as the expression of a literature of decadence and decomposition.[1] In the last study the question of the suicide of France is gravely discussed. The peril of death is discovered in the movement. Those who expose us to danger are Zola, Renan, Bourget, Daudet, and Maupassant. And yet however lofty the seat from which it was hurled, the anathema did not stay the invading tide. The term " nineties," used on the other side of the Channel to designate the English writers of that generation, has none the less become the synonym for a literature set free from " Mid-Victorian " servitudes. Hubert Crackanthorpe wrote with satisfaction in the *Yellow Book* of July, 1894 : " The truth must be admitted : the roar of unthinking prejudice is dying away."

Thus one always notes this occurrence of the same interval of ten years between French Naturalism and its repercussion in England. In Paris the movement was already somewhat ebbing since the appearance in 1887 of the famous Manifesto of the Five in the *Figaro*. It amounted in a measure to the " mea culpa " of certain of Zola's disciples. Finally in 1889 appeared the *Disciple*, in more than one respect the document of an accuser.

At the moment when in Great Britain these furious attacks against the new school were about to come to an end, the balance-sheet of that artificial literature, which had regularly poured forth upon the English public its three volume works, the famous " Three Deckers," was already drawn up. A cruel

1 *Quarterly Review*—The Modern French Novel, April 1890; Realism and Decadence in French Fiction, July 1890; English Realism and Romance, October 1891; The French Decadence, April 1892.

light was thrown upon the emptiness of those " eau de
rose " and orange-blossom intrigues. Rudyard
Kipling even wrote an ironical funeral ode upon the
" Three Deckers."

The reaction now set in. The battle was, in fact,
almost won. But it was not yet over. The Oscar
Wilde scandal (1895) had not yet occurred! Moreover, in 1898, nine years after the Vizetelly affair,
the publication of *Sexual Inversions* by Havelock
Ellis, was to be accompanied by new incidents. The
bookseller, George Bedborough, was imprisoned for
having sold a copy of this book to a detective in disguise. And yet the volume had been sold in sufficiently unusual circumstances, in a private house,
allowing of no kind of advertising. The work was
entirely devoid of licentious characteristics. It was
rather a treatise designed for the use of psychologists
or doctors and set forth in a technical language.
Facts like these explain how it was that attacks could
still be delivered in a certain form upon Hardy's
novels. The writer often refers to them in his
prefaces, thus shewing how sensitive he was to them.
There is a feminine public with which every man of
letters must reckon. If he neglects to take certain
precautions, an author exposes himself to miscalcula-
tions. Many feminine susceptibilities were treated
with scanty respect in his work and many woman-
readers found in numerous pages insults to their sex
and to their race.[1] In defiance of the ordinary conventions, so deeply rooted in England, Hardy presents Tess as an image of purity, when life had so

[1] See the often-quoted article of Mrs Oliphant, " The Anti-
Marriage League," in Blackwood's Magazine of January 1896, and
J. M. Barrie's pages on Thomas Hardy, " The Historian of
Wessex ", in the *Contemporary Review* of July 1889.

roughly thrust the girl aside from the ordinary tracks marked out by morality and religion. At that time, however, it was accepted as an unwritten law that the hero should receive his punishment as the reward of his crimes. Contrary to accepted tradition nothing of the kind occurs in Hardy. Tess is punished without herself being in fault, and therein Hardy made an innovation, in contempt of the conscientious scruples dear to his compatriots. From that hour dates the misunderstanding between them and him. Now, however, Hardy is largely outstripped, and after so long a period of reserve, English literature has caught up again with James Joyce, D. H. Lawrence, and Aldous Huxley, a fact which testifies to a profound evolution. The circumstance that Hardy's ashes now lie in Westminster Abbey is another and irrefutable proof of a change of attitude.

It may seem to have been in consequence of the reception accorded to *Jude the Obscure*, published in 1895, that Hardy abandoned the novel as a means of expression and returned to poetry. Like the *Esther Waters* of George Moore, this book was for a long time proscribed by the circulating libraries. Happily, defenders like Havelock Ellis came forward, proudly to take up the charge of immorality. Besides, the English public must be understood. For a long time many of our common-places remained on the other side of the Channel matters dissembled under the cloak of euphemism. Girl-mothers and free unions belonged to the category of shameful realities, hidden beneath veils arranged by cunning hands. Literature had not been assigned the task of supplying them with that publicity which sometimes renders vice attractive.

Like all Puritans even a Bernard Shaw is conscious
of a certain feeling of repugnance when speaking of
the physical aspect of love. He approaches it as if
it were an improper and shocking subject. That is
a true racial characteristic.

The author of *The Dynasts* was fully conscious of
the false prudery of these reticences. When, in that
epic drama, the Prince of Wales and his mistress,
Mrs Fitzherbert, appear in the house of the Marchion-
ess of Salisbury, the Spanish delegates present think
that this disorderly court strangely recalls that in
which the intriguer Godoy pushed his fortunes. An
Englishman explains to him : " Only you sin with
naked faces, and we with masks."[1] Nothing shews
more clearly the extent to which sexual problems
were calculated to cause an impression of embarrassment to the public across the Channel. It feels ill
at ease in the presence of episodes where angel and
beast confront one another and where the conventions
are relegated to the second place. In its eyes it is
not good taste to raise these questions. If one is
a gentleman, there are things of which one does not
speak.

If Hardy's work had not contained within it a
countervailing force in the fact that it was at the
same time the great pastoral symphony of the
Southern Counties, the well-bred man, the average
Englishman would have turned aside instinctively,
and it would have been injudicious to admire those
books or to admit such an admiration. For Hardy
was of those who live the life of a solitary, his feet
set proudly in a realm where his fellows might not

[1] *The Dynasts*, Part II, Act II, Scene III.

tread. So aloof an attitude could not fail to alienate men's minds.

Hardy brings to bear upon his heroes the concentrated forces of the influences of heredity and environment. He often explains the interplay of those forces, just as Taine disentangles in an author what is derived from time and what from environment. But with Hardy it is much more a mode of being than a system or doctrine, for this writer never makes an idea the rigid pivot of his art. He is led to adopt a pessimistic view of the world, but this view is in all respects correlative with his philosophical tendencies.

What answer can be made to his detractors, to those who vehemently reproach him with having no ethical sense, unless it be that on no occasion did he delight in obscenity in detail, or in licentious scenes? And yet (a fact which should surely leave no excuse for any kind of hypocrisy) in England eroticism has always supplied the material for an entire trade in clandestine literature. With a somewhat haughty regard for sincerity the novelist will know nothing of any concession to vulgarity, thus escaping those charges of immorality which needlessly alarmed consciences have been so ready to lavish upon him.

Having shewn the historical roots of the relationship connecting Hardy with certain tendencies of his generation, we must now determine the exact degree of his indebtedness to the Realist and Naturalistic movements in France and England. In the absence of that pure Realism which attributes to the external world the structure of a work of art (of which we find no traces in Hardy), an author may employ a Realistic technique to express the characteristics of the individual. This we encounter in Hardy. His affinity with certain members of the Naturalistic school and his indebtedness to Zola and also to Balzac reveal themselves in the first place by a frequent use of the scientific method in treating certain questions, in particular love. The numerous comparisons which he draws from physical life or from the exact sciences at times contribute to give his work that aspect of rigorous exactness which brings it into touch with the school of the author of *La Terre*, who so much desired to be the Claude Bernard of literature, to make of the novel a document of social and human history, and himself to remain the " Recorder of an Age." On the other hand, there are many traits which differentiate Hardy's descriptive technique from that of Zola. For Hardy the document, the type in detail is not an item to be seized upon deliberately, as if one were drawing up a description for the police. With him each point recorded proceeds from an observer who has looked upon things from the same intimate standpoint as, it may be, a woodman, a shepherd, or a hay-maker. But it is by the subsequent interpretation that he invests them with a wide application, with an impressive force and with the poetic element never absent from a moving revelation of truth.

Another trait which distinguishes Hardy from the main body of the Naturalistic army is a Romantic gift of conferring an anthropomorphic existence upon cosmic elements, of bestowing upon events the imprint of an implacable and almost eschatological direction. In him there is something of the visionary who perceives the process of becoming in the world, of the mystic who holds an unknowable, transcenden-

tal secret, the very antipodes of vulgar materialism.
An additional factor which separates him still further
from Naturalism is that aspect of his plots which
recalls the serial. In this respect Hardy is behind his
times. The out-of-date formula which he continues
to use has been abandoned by the new school. This
element in his work has its influence upon the Odyssey
of the human pair and will later on form the subject
of a special chapter.

On the other hand, as we have already indicated,
the undeniable trace of the Naturalistic theories, set
forth in Zola's *Le Roman Expérimental*, appears in
the importance accorded by Hardy to environment as
the determinant of the evolution of a character or of
a situation. As a representative of that influence
Egdon Heath plays a very definite role in *The Return
of the Native*. It contributed to the formation of the
characters. It appears as the paramount cause, giving rise to all the evils of which the heroes are to
taste. This wild stretch of country seemed to have
extended its vault above the heads of many who dwelt
within its confines. In other novels the encirclement
by things produces no less conclusive results.[1]

Another and equally certain symptom of the same
influence appears in the depicting of pathological
cases, such as those of Jude, of Arabella and of Sue;
recalling the Naturalistic school's taste for abnormal
types, like those which supplied Charcot with his
patients at the Salpètrière during his famous experi-
ments (1866-72).

---

[1] " Amid the oozing fatness and ferments of Froom Vale, at a
season when the rush of juices could almost be heard below the hiss
of fertilization, it was impossible that the most fanciful love should
not grow passionate. The early hearts existing here were impregnated by their surroundings." *Tess of the d'Urbervilles.*

In the land of Pickwick with his plethoric, childlike laugh, an attitude of deference towards philosophical schools will never be popular. The grim and outspoken pessimism of a Hardy will only penetrate in the guise of an intruder, tolerated rather than welcome. However representative and distinguished on the other side of the Channel the followers or associates of Realism or Naturalism may have been, they remained for the public at large distinct from the general run, too cerebral and a thought " wicked," to retain the English word with all that it implies. Their welcome, curious rather than heartfelt, procured them for a long time the position of imported articles, always the subject of discussion. In spite of his undeniable debt to Naturalism, Hardy cannot be brought within the category of a mere disciple. The creator of Jude and Tess, moreover, refused to admit his subjection to these influences, while on the other hand he is of those writers who do not fit readily into the framework of classification. At times he makes one think of certain forest trees which by their height and majesty dominate the whole forest and cause one to forget it.

In virtue of his Pantheistic outlook upon the world and of his taste for desolate spots Hardy is quite as much a Neo-Romantic.[1] Great enough to feel himself at ease in the kingdom of the elemental passions, he brings everything round to this object of his study, in a deliberate spirit of simplification.

At the end of the last century when the tendencies in literature were so profuse as at times to entail contradiction, it seemed right to place his name side

[1] Is there not an analogous mixture of Realism and Romanticism in Balzac too, in Flaubert also, and even in Zola?

by side with that of Swinburne, whose publishers
had withdrawn the *Poems and Ballads* from sale
fearing a public prosecution (1866). Swinburne in
his audacity went beyond the refinements of carnal
expression already scattered through the work of
Rossetti (*Nuptial Sleep*),[1] and the poet of *Laus
Veneris* shared with Hardy the honours of the
scandal. For sensual love is celebrated with enthusiasm by Swinburne, whose breath sweeps away
the poetry of " Virginibus puerisque," beloved of the
Victorians.[2]

Hardy, the pagan, who bestows life upon inanimate things, and Swinburne, the voluptuous
magician, who charms with words, linked, moreover,
by a real friendship, must stand together in virtue
of that new romantic splendour, with which they lent
radiance to the evening of the nineteenth century,
and of that battle which both upheld for the right
of speaking openly of the flesh.

In this essay the words Naturalism, Realism and
Neo-Romanticism have been deliberately placed in
the closest conjunction with one another. No one
of them would adequately explain the attitude of the
writer faced by the problem of sex. Truth and
poetry, science and vision continually mingle their
waters in the fountains haunted by his genius. No
formula more aptly expresses his art than the phrase

---

[1] Swinburne, Rossetti and William Morris were contemptuously
styled representatives of the " Fleshly School of Poetry." This
is the title of an article appearing in the *Contemporary Review*
of October 1871 (Robert Buchanan).

[2] Read in the " *Satires of Circumstance* " the homage charged
with emotions and memories paid by Hardy to Swinburne, " *A
Singer Asleep.*" Compare the invectives hurled at the unfeeling
god in " *Atalanta in Calydon* " with certain poems of Hardy and
their reproaches addressed to the deity.

of Zola : " A work of art is a corner of creation, seen through a temperament." The ego and the world ; the interdependence of these two factors explains the personality of his work and his sincerity. But no aspect of that work must ever be judged in isolation, if we would not misunderstand it or do it an injustice. To reproach Hardy on the ground of certain of his figures who are stained with animalism is to forget so many that are dream-products, pure women whose profile he has engraved. And one feels that only a being who has greatly loved them can have left us these captivating visions. If harsher and sometimes baser portraits precede or follow their delicate medallions, it is only because Hardy remembered the brave counsel of Saint Jerome :

" If an offence come out of the truth, better is it that the offence come than that the truth be concealed."[1]

It is far better to shew to what depths those beings may sink who seek one another in efforts to realise the ideal and impossible pair than, to persevere in vain lies and empty intrigues.

Reality, even if pushed to excess, is a tonic in its own way. It breathes in the free air. Its features are bronzed by the winds and the sun. It knows not the odour of damp exhaled by ancient houses where the light never penetrates.

The noontide rays are beneficial, and none must proscribe them on the score of a few cases of sunstroke. It is of little real importance that a dozen retrograde spirits are outraged by a novel, if thousands of consciences derive strength from it. The author

[1] Explanatory note to the first edition of *Tess of the d'Urbervilles*."

responds to the expectation of readers thirsty for truth and wearied by so many pages of puerility. It is to them that he speaks.

Whether he would or no, Hardy belonged to that Victorianism to which he formed the energetic anti-dote. All the actions and interactions revealed in his book bear the stamp of that epoch too clearly for it not to recognise him as one of its children, and pall-bearers.

CHAPTER III

PHILOSOPHICAL THOUGHT IN HARDY'S WORK AND
SEXUAL PESSIMISM

" The whole earth, continually saturated with
blood, is but one vast altar whereon all that lives
must be sacrificed, in a sacrifice that knows no
limit, no measure and no intermission, until the
final consummation, until the extinction of evil,
until the death of Death itself."

JOSEPH DE MAISTRE,
Soirées de Saint-Petersbourg.

WITH Hardy the comprehension, or better
expressed, the conception of the pair is
closely bound up with the philosophical
ideas contained in his literary effort. Everywhere
the author discovers the active and sovereign presence
of a force indifferent to the feelings of man. Regardless of good and evil, this force directs man and guides
his destiny, like the Wyrd in Beowulf. Upon those
who must sojourn here it conveys an impression of
spiritual solitude. Close at hand or standing afar off
it bears them down with the weight of its yoke and
with the threat of its persecutions. Throughout the
work we see the outlines of a world conceived of as
devoid of plan. It is a rich universe, the playground
of mighty energies which in their totality constitute
a system charged with dynamic force, but revealing

35

no vestige of a final aim. In this universe man is the plaything of an unexplained determinism. He fights instinctively for his species and hearkens only for an occasional moment to the appeals and suggestions of an intelligence which finds its purpose enshrined in the individual. On the other hand, the conflicts between the actions of every being and external events proclaim themselves as never ending and always fraught with suffering. Must one then become fatalist, do obeisance to the " fatum " of the ancient world or take refuge in Nihilism ? To act or to love is always to suffer, for it implies desire. And to desire is to struggle and to suffer. Such is the lot of humanity.

In many of his poems[1] and particularly in his great work, *The Dynasts*, Hardy asks himself, what is the meaning of the world ? Creation has no answer to offer. Ever silent it leaves him in his distress to confront the mysteries of destiny, the sport of chance and of external reality, amid which the individual and the " ego " take on outline and content, because they form part of the substance of the universe. Man stands faced with a mechanism which can pound him to atoms, without ever revealing the secret of its gear. He is at once witness and actor in a tragic affray which forces him, as a conscious being, to come to grips with the world of phenomena. Soon he learns the meaning of defeat and his sorry condition is revealed to him. With the same glance he beholds the futility of all striving, which may suggest to him, as in the terms of an ultimate teaching, a will to non-existence, the form in which he announces his abdication. Herein lies the explanation of the desire not

1 Poetic Works, *passim—Hap* (*Wessex Poems*), *Nature's Questioning* (*Wessex Poems*).

to transmit to other beings the fatal torch of life. In what is undoubtedly his most didactic book, *Jude the Obscure,* he proclaims this negative conclusion regarding the final outcome of the relations between man and woman. Too sincere to accept illusory panaceas, Hardy can only depict and testify to the unending conflict which opposes our desires and our will as individuals to an unseen and unfeeling power, mistress of destiny and of the world. At times that power recalls Nemesis, whose features announce vengeance, the implacable goddess whom every wrong-doer must bear within him for the redemption of his misdeeds and for the tragic consummation of his destiny.

What then is the use of shutting ourselves up within the limits of a captious sentimentality? Let us, rather, show that even in love the moments of happiness are only chance oases which we traverse in the twinkling of an eye : such moments as Angel and Tess will know in their passage along a road which leads to the gallows. Thus to all the injustices is added that of the final punishment inflicted by society. For the rest, if love is indeed the point upon which all human relations converge, in this study the writer will show no signs of exaggerated scrupulosity in his search for the truth, nor direct his researches with too penetrating a glance.

" *Candour in English Fiction,*"[1] such is the title of an article in which Hardy denounces hypocrisy. His genius dealt a mortal blow at that bad form of art. Under the impulse of this powerful brain the world spreads itself out before us, and many aspects of it reveal themselves without the author ever being

[1] " New Review " (1890).

able to take up a pragmatic attitude in the face of
the facts. Hostile to all forms of compromise with
their inaccessible ideal, the writer and his heroes alike
remain victims of their fundamental inability to
adapt themselves.

The representation of the human pair would remain
incomplete and fragmentary if it lacked that philosophical setting which, with all its woeful outlook,
lacks neither grandeur nor strength. Hardy's gaze
is so piercing that it discovers forces in realms to
which our eyes may not penetrate. For, in very
truth, above those conflicts impalpable powers seem
to rear themselves. Such are the new deities per-
ceived by the poet amid the inextricable confusions
of the influences at work within the universe. The
eternal and mysterious process of its becoming, its
unheeding mechanism and unending movement give
birth to deeds entailing suffering. De Vigny's lines
inevitably suggest themselves: " Live, frigid Nature,
live anew and unceasingly beneath our feet, there
where our thoughts may not penetrate, for it is your
law. Live and, if you are divine, pour out your scorn
upon man, the humble wayfarer, who deems himself
your king.''[1]

When similarities in thought reveal likeness in
temperament, comparisons are not merely permissible; they become necessary. De Vigny's pessimism comes first in time, before that of Hardy.
These two impersonal poets suffered, each from the

[1] La Maison du Berger.

Vivez, froide nature, et revivez sans cesse
Sous nos pieds, sous nos fronts, puisque c'est votre loi.
Vivez et dédaignez, si vous êtes déesse,
L'homme, humble passager, qui crut vous être roi.

" eternal silence of the divine."[1]   But in the eyes of
the one it is an honour to suffer in silence, for he is a
Stoic. The other is more a metaphysician; he does
not profess that philosophy of suffering. From his
star-bound observatory Hardy discovers an all-
devouring phenomenalism, the decline of which he
only descries in the distance of the remote future.

In its sombre objectivity this writer's genius rises
to a personification of phenomena. Things, trees,
moors or ancient towers become living beings or
rather personalities. And, as counterpart, human
beings, inanimate things and natural forces communicate with one another by an incessant process of
osmosis and seem to bestow their own hues upon one
another. Hardy's work is penetrated by this Pantheism. It is impregnated with it just as the tourney
of Good and Evil and the contest of Light and
Darkness form the substance of the *Légende des
Siecles*.

The perception of the mechanism which dominates
the world might lead to an entirely materialistic explanation of things. For that will, which Hardy
discovers, he presents to us as a lifeless force in *The
Dynasts* and in many of his poems. But, on the
other hand, we end with transcendentalism, with the
concept of a monistic universe, swayed by a will to
power. Upon the shoulders of a strange despot, unconscious and unwearying, Hardy lays the responsibility for those ills and sufferings, the outcome of
which is pure loss. This monstrous automaton which
constitutes the Immanent Will is made to appear on
the scene in the over-world of *The Dynasts*:

1 *The Origin of Species*, 1859.

" The Will has woven with an absent heed
     Since life first was; and ever will so weave."[1]

Such a metaphysical hypothesis offers points of
striking resemblance to the conceptions of Schopenhauer, as set forth in his treatise : " Die Welt als Wille
und Vorstellung," and throughout the whole of his
work.

This issue has given rise to controversy. To what
extent was Hardy subject to the influence of the
German philosopher ? The letter from Sir Edmund
Gosse to Mr Hedgcock, published in the volume from
the latter's pen, merely shows that in 1874 Hardy
knew nothing of Schopenhauer, and that the ideas
which had made it possible to connect him with the
thinker from beyond the Rhine were already present
in his thought and had even found expression. We
are not concerned to deny—far from it—the strange
similarity of tendencies represented by these two
minds. Such encounters are too rare and too extra-
ordinary not to provoke comment.

As Mr Brennecke, however, tells us in *Hardy's
Universe,*"[2] the poet admitted on several occasions
the influence exercised upon him by Schopenhauer.
Quite apart from this avowal, *The Dynasts* contains
a whole terminology, borrowed from Schopenhauer
(see Mr Hedgcock's book, page 392), and this second
proof is conclusive.

Helen Garwood, who studied Hardy's work as an
expression of the philosophy of Schopenhauer, made
an effort to reach a definite position on this point :
" How far Schopenhauer is responsible for this attitude of Hardy seems, at present, a question which

1 *The Dynasts* Forescene.
2 See page 14.

can be limited, but not answered.   One must await a fuller biography or an autobiographical statement. The mention of Schopenhauer in *Tess*, and in a letter to the Academy concerning Maeterlinck's *Apology for Nature*, justifies the assumption that he is at least familiar with the works of that philosopher.   In a letter, however, which he very courteously sent me in answer to my inquiry, Mr Hardy speaks of his philosophy being a development from Schopenhauer through later philosophers."

Hardy had no need to borrow this pessimism, already condensed in pieces like *Hap*, written after his twenty-fifth year.   It was already his secret doctrine, his *vade mecum*, and perhaps he did nothing beyond taking possession of it, as of an estate, speedily to be improved, from the Biblical sources of the world's sadness.   Later, as we shall see further on, he was able to read those who continued or popularised the work of Schopenhauer.

Hardy, the philosophical poet, found anew in Schopenhauer, the poetic philosopher, his own substance and drew nourishment from it.   He found anew his own thought at a more highly developed stage, but with the addition of that powerful charm issuing from the artistic temperament of Schopenhauer.   Both were prophets of the Immanent Will. And in both cases it is less the philosophy itself than the epic rigour of its expression which is of moment.

It would no doubt be fruitless to seek for any rigorous definition of the exact part played by this influence. The mere fact of being impalpable does not always deprive an influence of decisive effect.   All that is needed for its full transmission is a combination of not very numerous but really adequate causes.

When garnered by an eager mind a single quotation may have more effect than a whole volume.

It must, moreover, be noted that Hardy was, as is proved by the constant references which occur in his work, too great a reader to shrink from frequently tracing his thought back to the very sources of pessimism.   Some days before his death he caused passages of Omar Khayyam once more to be read to him.

The representation of the universe, such as one finds it in the works of the philosopher of Frankfort, reappears in the poet who evoked the epic of Napoleon. The essence of things in themselves is never known.   Our senses are only intermediaries, informers whose powers and acuteness are limited; and we reconstruct the world on the basis of these fragile and sometimes erroneous data. Our universe is only a cerebral phenomenon. We owe it to consciousness, that bloom of mere contingency, which has surely flowered to our misfortune. But was not the idea of the consciousness gradually penetrating the universe, as if to regenerate and save it, probably borrowed by Hardy from von Hartmann?

Beneath these forms, whether stubborn and taciturn or passionate and exuberant, the will to live exists everywhere in the world. Its presence may be observed in the mineral and vegetable kingdoms. Favoured by instincts, its force becomes intensified in the animal until it reaches its bursting point in man, whose brain, an admirable instrument for directing action, often comes to its aid. This philosophy, so close to that of Schopenhauer, is less a system of ideas than a vision of things, the vision of an artist gifted with the power of understanding the world. This interpretation of the universe, intuitive rather than rationalistic, leads straight to agnosticism.

The writer always remained a tenacious questioner, bending a hypnotic gaze upon appearance and its misleading tokens, sometimes trying to penetrate the secret of those two forms of our thought, space and time.

Hardy's attitude towards the problem of religion is probably already contained in these philosophical premises. Religion originates in the metaphysical need which man feels for elucidating the mysteries of existence and death.

It was probably about 1860, during the long stay which he made in London, to develop his architectural knowledge, that Blomfield's[1] pupil lost his faith. This was just the period when the controversy between the partisans of science and the defenders of theology was raging most fiercely.

The verses which Hardy wrote at the age of twenty-six express the full extent of the divorce between religion and the conception of a world unheeding and of evil intent, utterly void of providence. As M. Valéry Larbaud[2] so justly describes it, the discussion assumes the form of a *personal quarrel with God.* Hardy was never to depart from this attitude. Treading all respect under foot, he did not fear to write such poems as " Panthera " and " In St Paul's a While Ago," wherein the insults showered upon Christianity reach the point of blasphemy. And yet for Hardy himself doubt and incredulity were never

1 Sir Arthur Blomfield, architect, who reconstructed the actually existing nave of Saint Saviour's, Southwark, was one of the English architects most successful in imitating the medieval builders.
2 Ce Vice Impuni, La Lecture, Valéry Larbaud, Study of *The Dynasts.*

to alleviate uneasiness. Bitter despair is the child of
negation hanging over the world like a dark shadow.

There is no doubt that in *Two on a Tower* one encounters an unfriendly criticism of the ecclesiastical
type, and in *Far From the Madding Crowd* a biting
criticism of dogma, irreverences which betray a kind
of anti-religious fanaticism, possibly inculcated by
the reading of Gibbon. But it would assuredly offend
against the deeper side of his work and of his philosophy in this place to probe too deeply into the
analysis of these points and these attacks. The
underlying tendency is derived from the polemic of
his age. Like many Englishmen Hardy is an exe-
getic, but, unlike Englishmen, he has a second
personality, that of a Voltairean.

His position towards that problem derives its inspiration from certain ideas which can easily be
re-assembled in a few words. Strict observance did
not in his eyes represent the essential element contained in dogmas. There are absolute principles of
justice and goodness enthroned above the ritual
itself. Surely the letter must be rejected where it
runs counter to the spirit, and orthodoxy when it
contradicts reason. There are times when it is necessary to cut away chance shoots, in order that the
plant itself may remain.

We see once more that the general movement of
thought, in Hardy's case too, followed the rhythm set
by his age.

Reaching their zenith about 1860, the doctrines of
utilitarianism and evolution and freedom of thought,
as represented by John Stuart Mill, Darwin, Spencer,
and Huxley, poured forth a mighty hymn of optimism. Science had relegated the old dogmas to the

" penetralia " of museums and libraries. But however symbolic, these gestures very thinly disguised their own final process of reduction to a peremptory doctrine of materialism. At the very moment which seemed to promise an era of boundless conquest to the human spirit, so many hopes began to grow dim. The voice of Herbert Spencer was not yet silent, when the sound of lamentations was already making itself heard.[1]

Darwin's book on the origin of species contained within itself all the elements of a reaction. The struggle for existence and the survival of the fittest ? This was a proclamation of very stern theories. The whole panorama of economic life seemed to confirm them, and there was place within them for the idea of the inevitable and for the doctrine of " laissez-faire."

Germany, upon whose soil the philosophy of the Will and of the Unconscious had found its seed-ground with Edward von Hartmann, Haeckel, and Schopenhauer, was to become the classic land of a pessimism of which Heine was perhaps the first victim. Side by side with the masters the names of Bahnsen, Taubert, and Frauenstaedt must be mentioned. Each in his own way gives expression to the idea of a world the causes of which are unintelligible. The Unconscious becomes the absolute subject, comprising within itself the substance, the ego, the idea and the energy existing throughout the universe.

The evil germ was transmitted from one country to another, wherever the presence of similar predispositions in different spiritual climates permitted of

1 In France radiant confidence in progress began to cool down towards 1850. This is another example of the regularity of that interval of about ten years between French thought and the movement of ideas on the other side of the Channel.

the formation of convergent currents. The study of these manifestations is indispensable to the formation of any adequate conception of a movement of ideas.

At the beginning of the century, England, the home of the gloomy Burton, had given birth to T. L. Beddoes, who seems to have been persecuted by the idea of death to the point of suicide. A genius tortured, pathetic and macabre, sailing under the colours of German Romanticism, he was only a forerunner. Moreover, his influence was slow to make itself felt; *Death's Jest Book* was only published in 1850. In Matthew Arnold metaphysical uneasiness appears in *Dover Beach* and *Human Life*. There is again *The City of Dreadful Night* of James Thompson with its strange despair. At that time, after 1860, there existed in England a veritable " Pleïade " of poets of doubt and suffering;[1] Arthur Hugh Clough, the friend of Matthew Arnold, and Edward Fitzgerald.[2] This culminating moment of a terrible dismay in European thought which found its most striking expression in Schopenhauer was to have its repercussion, above all in England, after 1870, in a series of philosophical books and essays.[3] In France its greatest voices were Lecomte de Lisle and perhaps Baudelaire. In Russia it produced Nihilism, whose shroud was thrown about so many books, soon widely

[1] Even in Tennyson one often hears an unquiet tone. " *In Memoriam* " (1850):

> " But what am I?
> An infant crying in the night,
> An infant crying for the light,
> And with no language but a cry."

[2] The translator of Omar Khayyam.

[3] Cf. Helen Zimmern, whose book on Schopenhauer dates from 1876, and James Sully, author of " *Pessimism* " (1877), " *The World as Will and Idea*," translated by R. B. Haldane (1883-86).

circulated in translation. About 1895, when Hardy's last novels were appearing, English decadence, personified by Oscar Wilde, reached its zenith. Disgust at life and Realism in its crudest form displayed themselves in *The Yellow Book*, to which all the " fin de siècle " writers contributed. In this periodical and similarly in *The Savoy* the tendencies seemed at times divergent, but they might all have been said to represent the reign of Aubrey Beardsley, the most prominent among their illustrators, the master of a daring and merciless pencil. This period coincides with the first signs of faltering in the onward movement of Great Britain's economic progress and with the earliest uncertainties aroused by foreign competition.

Now, however, that we have outlined the contemporary influences that may have acted upon Hardy, it is no less expedient to show—although in a necessarily incomplete form, on account of the impatient reserve which he maintained upon the subject—how far his personal experiences may have contributed to form his thought. As has been pointed out, his earliest verses already gave expression to the lofty despair of a poet, who perceives the tragedy which darkens the enigma of life and who suffers under the appalling indifference of things, and above all at the role assigned to chance, that unconscious headsman. The challenges with which he at times apostrophises the irresponsible First Cause resound with the note of passionate grief such as we hear in verses of the Old Testament. In the writer there reappears the man, perhaps too the child, who has read Job and Jeremiah. Thus when he took his first soundings of the universe, Hardy discovered abysses. And yet for his thought to have assumed that form, must there not have lain within him some germ deeply implanted, the off-spring of atavism or chance?

Why should we regard this inborn sadness merely as an original gift of his nature?

Like many of his characters Hardy was the last of a family fallen from its ancient estate. The Hardys came from Jersey in the fifteenth century. They knew prosperity. An inscription in the church of St Peter in Dorchester tells of the donation of a benefactor in the sixteenth century, Thomas Hardy of Melcombe Regis. The family also gave Admiral Hardy, commander of the " Victory " at Trafalgar, whom the poet introduces in *The Dynasts*.

The eldest of four children, our Thomas Hardy is the only one who married. And he died childless. He really may be said to have incarnated the end of a stock. Until the age of six he was himself so sickly that his parents thought he could not live. As his second wife, Mrs Florence Hardy, who is also his biographer, tells us, once at the age of only ten or twelve, he was sleeping stretched out in the sun when, with a feeling of intense bitterness, he suddenly became conscious of the futility of his life. He felt himself to be the end of the race.

Hardy is autochthonous. His lonely childhood was passed in the hamlet of Upper Bockhampton, where he was born in a thatched cottage, some three miles from Dorchester, on the edge of that wild heath, from which he derived inspiration for Egdon Heath. From his earliest wanderings, across the moors, where orchards cling about hamlets and farmsteads, the child brought back a dazzling vision of a Nature, that yet was cruel and insensible. All around stood, testifying to the past, Celtic, Roman, Danish, Saxon,

Gothic, Elizabethan or Georgian, Druidical stones,
amphitheatres, tumuli, earth fortifications, abbeys,
manor-houses, barns, inns or the residences of
noblemen. And all these relics told, without explaining or justifying, of the persistent effort of humanity,
unceasing and ever fraught with suffering. It is like
the perfume of a funeral pyre, rising from the soil
of Wessex, where he played, like Clym, on Egdon
Heath, when the young shoots of his genius were
first appearing. Thus was born the pessimism of a
proud and tender heart which throughout life continued jealous of rendering up its secrets. Grafted
upon one who had to deplore neither poverty nor
neglect, this sentiment was throughout the whole of
the writer's career to retain the marks of an intellectual origin. A shy pride always continued to dwell
within the depths of his being. As Mr G. K.
Chesterton has well pointed out in his *Dickens*, it is
not those who have themselves known misfortune,
whose philosophy of life remains bitter. The outlook
of the wretched upon life is too narrow for them to
criticize or to curse it! Aristocrats, like Byron or
Swinburne, give the stuff of which pessimists are
made.

Hardy was brought up by a mother of some
distinction, who guided his earliest studies and
awakened his tastes. The son of a contractor, the
young man was first of all destined for the Church,
then for the profession of architecture. It was with
a view to preparing himself for this profession that
he came to live in Dorchester. The associations which
he formed in that town during the three years spent
with Mr Hicks, a restorer of churches, were not without influence upon his thought. A friend made him

acquainted with the Greek tragedians. The architect's pupil also became intimate with a journalist[1]
and with theological students. The future writer,
who, like Rousseau, remained in some sense a self-
taught man, then experienced the prestige of culture.
He sought contact with those privileged men, whose
lives were devoted to the jousts of the intellect. But
the development of his own understanding was never
to lose that element of hastiness, oddness and incom-
pleteness. The writer always retained the respect of
a Jude for that learning which he had acquired with
so much difficulty. He was very proud of the distinctions which several English universities had
conferred upon him, and, when he was laid in his
coffin to be cremated at Woking, he was wrapped in
the crimson robe of an Honorary Fellow. By the very
multiplicity of the heroes, in whom he has incarnated
the thirst for learning, Hardy, the man of the heaths
and the woods, evoked the uneasiness and ignorance
of humanity, turned towards learning. He also
showed that that new religion has no balm within
its teaching apt to the healing of every wound.

What, to begin with, is knowledge? The latter-
day chimera whose siren voice sometimes carries enchantment, but does not always bring peace of heart
and spirit.

"How fares the truth now?—Ill?
Do pens but slily further her advance? "[2]

How should knowledge teach happiness when it has

1 Horace Moule, then at the beginning of his literary career, was
no doubt the original of the character of Henry Knight in " A
Pair of Blue Eyes." He died tragically in 1873, much to Hardy's
sorrow.
2 Poems of Pilgrimage. Poems of the Past and the Present.
Lausanne. In Gibbon's old garden.

not as yet discovered the meaning of truth? Let us
examine the lot of the intellectuals as depicted in the
Wessex Novels. What is the use of that fine culture
to Henry Knight?[1] He who extends the range of his
knowledge also increases his possibilities of suffering.
" Qui auget scientiam auget dolorem."

The " primitivist," therefore, inclines by preference towards rustic life. He looks upon those
peasants whose lives will never be smitten by the ills
born of thought. Must he not, like another Rousseau,
fear the effects of an artificial civilization? Fate
picks out the adepts of learning for her fiercest onsets,
whereas she respects those who remain in contact with
Nature.

When Hardy turns towards those servants of the
soil, a philosophy of wisdom and resignation mounts
aloft from his pages like the gentle haze which sometimes ascends in the wake of the plough-share. The
Stoic régime, as it is practised by the humble, can
alone satisfy the demands of existence. They know
from experience, those peasants, that evil is inseparable from life; that one must accept it and not break
oneself to pieces in striving against it.

The whole of this philosophy is far more the natural
expression of an artist's and thinker's temperament
than the doctrinal co-ordination of views on the
universe. Moreover, the writer always sets his face
against presenting a system in the sense congenial
to a theorist. Not, indeed, that tendencies towards
cohesion are entirely absent. This rough apanage of
ideas and concepts, which form the substance of the
Wessex Novels and *Poems*, and, above all, of *The*

[1] *A Pair of Blue Eyes.*

Dynasts, makes it possible to reconstruct a real metaphysical system.

In the preface written in 1922 to *Late Lyrics and Earlier* Hardy takes up the challenge. He denies that he is a pessimist and avows his belief in a slow evolution towards better things. He associates himself with evolutionary Pantheism.

Moreover, he always rose up in protest, whenever a critic sought to couple with his name the epithet of pessimist and to make him the disciple of any definite school.

Again this pessimist has the gift of pity and sympathy which he extends to all human beings, to the lowest animals and to plants themselves. None of his characters are really odious. His creatures are fallible beings, guided by destiny and heredity, victims of their own characters and moulded by all the forces of the environment.

From those rugged heights from which Determinism dominates the world the problem of evil no longer appeared from the same angle.

According to the definition of the critic Duffin, in Hardy's eyes, " Life is a lost, inglorious and bloody battle."[1]

To associate with these books is an excellent schooling for those brave spirits who are not afraid of the unescapable revelation of all the vicissitudes that may be foreseen. If it entailed nothing more than this training in resignation, it would have been in this spirit that Hardy pronounced his last word. But this interpretation would not have received the assent of a poet, many of whose verses seem to open a door

[1] *Thomas Hardy*, H. C. Duffin Ch. IV, pt. II, p. 208.

upon something other than evil. Does he not seek
to justify by these revealing words all the misad-
ventures endured throughout so many pages:

> " . . . . If a way to the Better there be, it
> exacts a full look at the Worst."[1]

The poem containing these verses appeared in 1901,
but as the poet declares in the preface to *Late Lyrics
and Earlier* it had been written earlier (1895-1896).

Like his contemporary, A. E. Housman, Hardy
celebrates this virtue that lies in pessimism, representing it as a bitter herb, but as a herb which may
cure.

In a measure his pessimism is even a precautionary
pessimism, a buckler, a palladium. It is the provision made by a far-sighted mind, capable of
profiting in advance by the lessons of adversity.

The pessimism of Leopardi, on the other hand,
seems on the whole to have been derived from the
misfortunes which filled his life, from ill-health and
from domestic annoyances. In his own life lay the
justification of the judgment which he pronounced
upon life. Such was not the case with Hardy.

One must bow before the corrections with which
he has himself attenuated some of the most bitter
of his plaints.

One realises in the presence of this newly gained
calm the errors to which anyone would expose himself who sought to pass judgment in terms of vigorous
generalities. For clearly though its structure is outlined, this work remains a living organism in process
of evolution. Its cells unceasingly drift among

---

[1] In Tenebris. II, *Poems of the Past and the Present.*

phagocytes and microbes engaged in perpetual strife in those centres where evil has summoned them. The issue is not always fatal. The possibility of alternative conclusions leads one from the shades of radical negation to the wan, pallid light of a dawn, which may perhaps become the light of day.

Sometimes during civil wars a truce must be arranged in order to carry away the dead, heaped up on both sides of the barricade. The next day in the city the wounded are counted, the uninjured meet and the enemies of the day before are reconciled. Such conventions intervene in Hardy's pages, their melancholy labour seeming to resemble the work of some magical healer, sent by Providence. Gabriel will no doubt be happy with Bathsheba, Farfrae with Elisabeth-Jane. One imagines them reaching the age of Philemon and Baucis in their felicity, but it is merely a dream that one pursues.

Coggan, one of those peasants whose rule in life lies in absolute submission to fate, an obstinate and inborn confidence in the presence in things of restorative powers, expresses this philosophy of consolation which humble members of the crowd often set forth more effectively than the principal actors in the drama. He is but one of the voices in the choir which plays its role throughout *Far From the Madding Crowd*. Yet he passes a just sentence upon that hermetically sealed pessimism to which some of the novels might give currency. " Hurrah," he cries on seeing a misfortune averted, " God's above the devil yet."

This utterance contains the word *in fine*. It is the utterance of a simple peasant, who sees the whole folly of certain gestures and perceives half-way up those slopes, that are without steepness, the road leading to wisdom and surely also to a healthy consciousness, a future emergence upon a world set free.

Hardy's pessimism is, in virtue of this atmosphere, much more an eradicator of illusions than an infectious prompting to despair. In spite of heart-rending conclusions, the writer's balance is safe-guarded, and even the orderly arrangement of his work attests it. It is in the joy of the eyes, the ardent pleasure of the glance that the incomparable landscape artist found his counterpoise. Hand in hand with his sombre faith went a prodigious faculty for exhilaration amid the fairest spectacles of nature.

And, he who, dwelling apart in his house amid the fields, drew near to those simple beings whose virtues he celebrated, could not but have been one of the least unhappy of mortals in an imperfect world. Shunning that glory which might often have been a mere intruder, he banished artificiality from his life, that he might live worthily.

> " I never cared for Life;
> Life cared for me. . . ."[1]

If the artist and the thinker have found a bitter pleasure in groping their way along the path that leads to annihilation, they have at the same time known the gentler pleasures of irony and the harsh satisfaction of the man who has weighed everything in the balance. For in Hardy we meet the humorist filled with good nature and malice. The shrewd utterance of the coachman Dewy in *Under the Green-*

[1] Late Lyrics and Earlier. Epitaph.

wood Tree well expresses the scepticism, at once lucid and humorous, of his attitude towards " respectable " art and stories with happy endings.

" My sonnies, all true stories have a coarseness or a bad moral, depend upon't. If the story-tellers could ha' got decency and good morals from true stories, who'd ha' troubled to invent parables ? "

CHAPTER IV

THE CONFLICT OF THE SEXES

And she said yet further to me : " Do you not
know that love is a combat? Would you, the most
valiant among men, accept a triumph without ever
having given battle? "

JARDIN DES CARESSES.

AS a poet of unfulfilled destinies and human
failure, Hardy conceived of love and examined it in accordance with certain norms.
In this all important part of his work he embarks
upon a study of the human pair, which cannot but
stir and disquiet his readers.

The eyes of the pair are opened in the course of a
joust in which sensibilities are the combatants. A
conflict between two human beings is always the
grand climax in any sentimental crisis. From the
outset no single phase is wanting. Upon the high
warp tapestry presented by the hand of Hardy the
blood that streams from the wounds soaks through
the very woof, that woof which is itself the substance
of the destiny of two heroes. This is what is revealed
by the study of the conflict of the sexes.

Hardy follows up this study of the encounter with
the zeal proper to the visionary, whose glance penetrates to the heart of the upheaval constituting a
tragic situation. It is his favourite milieu. It pro-

vides him with that atmosphere in which, as M. Paul
Margueritte wrote in the preface to the translation
of *The Well-Beloved*, " things, gestures, and words
are prolonged to the infinite." Although the story
itself never slackens its pace, these decisive elements
are not permanently present. But the chapters which
prepare the crisis are followed by pages which start
up glowing with fire, those pages in which Hardy's
pair makes its appearance. Such are those preceding
the climax in *A Pair of Blue Eyes*, where Elfride and
Knight destroy for ever their chances of happiness.
Elfride's overwhelmed sincerity and Knight's prejudices become the sorry artisans which are to de-
fraud them of it. The drama rises to the full height
of its power during those intense moments. Human
littleness triumphs over love, because its malignity
gets the better of the generous forces of affection and
tenderness. Love continues unequal to its task and
remains at the mercy of events.

In such situations Hardy's characters take on their
true outline. Before them towers the dark and
malignant power of destiny. It is seen above the
heads of the pair, as though poised upon the sombre
and pitiless wings of some deity. One feels, one
divines its presence by presageful signs. " Some
fatality must be hanging over her head," it is said of
Elfride. Adversity bears her down under the excessive weight of her love and of her weakness, and
she contemplates the approach of misfortune with
trembling submission. For a harsh destiny wills that
at that instant and in the same place she shall again
live through an hour of love that she has already
known with another man, the architect's pupil,
Stephen Smith. Soon the past rises up to threaten

the present. The egoistic fiancé of to-day wishes to
find in Elfride a virgin soul. In the presence of her
whom he believes himself to love he wonders whether
the rock upon which they are seated has not sup-
ported other couples clasped in each other's arms.
The torturing memory of a past love begins to define
itself and exasperates Elfride. In future she is to be
nothing but the plaything of cruel circumstances that
bear the stamp of fatality. The girl discovers by the
aid of the sloping rays of the setting sun a lost jewel,
lying in the crack of the rock, and she is unfortunate
enough to make a clumsy allusion to that episode,
now invested with all the force of a denunciation.
And so Elfride is defeated, for that past love comes
to life again in her eyes, embodied in the lost ear-
ring which has now been found. A silent witness, it
rises before her in accusation. The avowals fall from
her lips like leaves from a stricken tree, shaken down
by the wind. She surrenders herself passively to a
series of admissions which leave her at the mercy of
misfortune. Unable to turn aside the menace which
advances upon her, having no other aid at hand but
her silence, she is sucked down into the terror that
besets her soul. Every word uttered by Elfride is
catastrophic in its effect upon Knight. He, too, will
soon give way, but to the limited suggestions offered
by his man's egoism. The dream is over. Two
scenes of love are set one upon the other in the same
place and their sentimental results are in some sort
destructive of one another. By a strange coincidence, two friends expel one another from the heart
of the same woman, shutting each other out from
the possibility of happiness. Henceforth the idyll
stands condemned. Such is the outcome of that halt

upon the lofty promontory, overlooking the sea. In the course of a few chapters that love will gradually be led up to its agony, for the machinery has already been set in motion to produce results which must make repudiation inevitable.

The story of this crisis has been retraced in these pages only for the purpose of providing a canvas which will make it easier to follow the pair throughout the series of duels which characterize these novels.

At the same time alike in the actors and in the events a savagery reveals itself, propitious to the work of destruction. This Satanic element of cruelty or of ferocious irony shows that love is born and runs its course in an atmosphere of struggle. There are encounters, there are moments when forces of attraction make themselves felt. There is the shock of contact. The woman and her lover are regarded as two elemental forces which complete one another, although they run counter to each other, two planets the mutual attraction of which, real although intermittent, is governed by obscure and inexorable laws. When these two beings confront one another, one has the impression that the " fatum " of the ancients haunts their path, and one feels that two fanatical warriors are about to struggle and to perish in contending for a harmony that can never be realised. The banding together in the circumstances of all the forces of irony and derision, of all the caprice that the vicissitudes of life can call forth lends hideous intensification to the fratricidal spirit with which this antagonism is filled. Love which desires and seeks for the union of the sexes becomes a combat, a struggle between the sexes. The weapons employed are cunning, lying, coquetry and seduction. The final stakes are the continued existence of the species or the egoistic satisfaction of the individual, two really irreconcilable antinomies. The lovers always continue enemies. Indeed, at the roots of such a love there ferments a hatred which may transform it into an opposite sentiment, if the obstacles which it encounters on its path prove too great. In love, as in the heart of Chimène, we sometimes meet with that conflict between instinct which bids one love and duty which announces hatred.

Did not Plato once compare a man's love to that of a wolf for the lamb which he devours?

It is of such elements that one must take account, if one would gain some idea of the conflict of the sexes. The duel cannot be understood apart from the psychological eddyings resulting from those spiritual conjunctions which imply so much surrender, but which actually reveal such a mass of egoism.

If Tolstoy's name has been mentioned in connection with the *Kreutzer Sonata*, those of Strindberg and Ibsen announce themselves no less peremptorily in a chapter dealing with the conflict of the sexes. The names of the two Scandinavians and of the mighty Slav cannot be separated from that of Hardy, when we approach this problem. In virtue of the spaciousness with which it is treated, of the atmosphere amid which it takes shape, this question appears in their work as the reflection of the same avowed pre-occupation, and as the anxiety to exhibit in the fullest possible light, however harsh it be, the whole drama of sexual life, all the forces which range themselves in combat in the persons of the pair and all the evils engendered by that juxtaposition of creatures, drawn together by their alleged complementary value.

Let us not seek for any absolute analogy of tendencies. Sufficiently striking is the fact of the encounter itself, which leads all these writers to embark upon the same theme, to handle it amid the panting of horses and the thunder of their hoofs in a furious gallop in which everything is trampled under foot.

With Ibsen it is a hand-to-hand conflict in which the woman strives to gain a social advantage over the man, to lay hands upon a supremacy which shall be real and concrete. A Hedda Gabler devours men like Laura in Strindberg (*The Father*). Each is in revolt. But the will to liberation which inspires *The Doll's House* finds its answer in Strindberg's terrific pamphlet against feminism.

The demoniacal element which in Hardy has its abode in events is transferred in Strindberg (*The Dance of Death*) to the characters. Within them rages the genius of evil, an epileptic fury of destruction.

What we see in Hardy is not so much the product of any given moment of a civilisation that is actually evolving. It is rather a conflict proceeding from the functional separation of the sexes and the collision that ensues. He examines the permanent, immovable, eternal aspect of sexual life, not merely the manifestations of its volcanic moments. With him the conflict becomes more human. It is not blunted by words or by actuality, by exceptional characters or by mere fashions in literature. The reader is present at every phase of the evolution of the conflict. From its inception to the final crisis the whole series of

stages passes in procession, each retaining its special
significance and its own form of eloquence.

In such a conflict there are, of course, skirmishing
encounters between the troops of the two vanguards.
The games of chess, played between Elfride and
Stephen and Elfride and Knight, reproducing the
same scenes in reversed situations, exemplify this
twice over.[1] For the simple encounter on the chess-
board veils a passage of arms of far deeper significance.

When Elfride and Stephen face one another, it is
the young woman who has the last word. In the
other encounters Knight is the victor, Elfride fleeing
from the field vanquished and humiliated. The sole
aim of these chess-parties is to mask the preliminary
assaults in the course of which each combatant quali-
fies himself before embarking upon the most dangerous encounter of all, from which the pact of love
proceeds. M. Charles du Bos refuses to see this
element of conflict in the relations between the
sexes as presented by Hardy. It may be, as the
eminent author of *Approximations* maintains, that
the man and the woman are not put before us in
opposition to one another, as completely autonomous personalities, asserting themselves to their
full extent. But the field is a vaster one, and
in the all-embracing whirlpool in which everything
is sucked down, the two chief characters themselves
are condemned by their instincts to meet but
in conflict, to seek for, but never to discover one
another, to grasp each other only in the grip of
strangulation, impelled by forces regardless of those
individual reactions which should forbid such a contest.

[1] " *A Pair of Blue Eyes* ", Chapters VII and VIII.

According to M. du Bos the conflict must be due to the dissociation between the sexual instinct and the instinct of love, when both take the field. It is surely difficult to make so radical a distinction in Hardy's characters, where the two tendencies are generally confounded, as in the case of Viviette Constantine. We return, therefore, tenaciously to the grimmer formula of the unending combat born of the differentiation of beings and of their functions.

In order to retain for love this character of a struggle developing between two individuals at the moment when the pair first comes into being and for as long as the union lasts, Hardy had to proceed with a discrimination that must never fail and to bring the two characters into opposition with one another in virtue of their own contrasted natures. " She " and " he " must, if one may so express it, incarnate different tendencies. The moral divergencies are accompanied by physical contradictions. In love the antagonisms are made to result from the discrepancies between ideals and the differences of type. In *Two on a Tower* this antithesis makes itself seen between the Shelley-like silhouette of the fair heaven-born Swithin and Viviette, whose languid nature and dark complexion veil an element of sensuality. In Hardy's work the two kinds of influence are not separate, for all converges upon the same end.

Yet while we note in certain characters that physical analogy, as it appears between Elfride and Stephen[1], the resemblance between them does not go very deep, the attraction resting upon a more fragile basis. Smith is a kind of masculine replica of Elfrida.

[1] *A Pair of Blue Eyes.*

Thus the pair which flatters itself that it is realising a unity is by the very laws of its own nature a duality. The two beings which it ought to unite confront one another, measuring each other's strength. A plant of natural growth, with her roots deeply set in heredity instincts, Tess is led by fate towards Alec, a voluptuary without scruples, then to Angel, a poor-blooded intellectual, almost contemptible in his enslavement to prejudice. Thus Hardy opposes this woman's innocence to the sensuality and egoism of the heir of upstarts, later her fidelity to the fickleness of the clergyman's son.

By one of the contraditions implicit in its destiny, the couple is faced with danger from the very moment of its coming into being. It is, therefore, called into existence, only to meet with immediate threats. In this fact resides the very spirit of Hardy's conception, all that is most essential and irreducible in it. But it is a conception shared by other writers, and M. Paul Souday has lately enshrined it in the following admirable formula: "Nature in her malevolence, while seeming to have need of the couple, almost always extends its scope, so that it becomes a triad. Like Verlaine in his *Art Poétique*, she prefers the odd number."[1]

With an increasing solicitude for composition, the writer assembles his heroes in groups of three, four, or at most five leading characters. The different types constituting these groups have their places allotted to them as in a picture by the interplay of opposing forces. One is conscious of the full measure of the art with which the author has fixed the balance of the characters within each group. In *The Wood-*

[1] Feuilleton Littéraire du Temps, 28 Mars 1929.

landers Winterborne, the planter of apple-trees, a true cavalier, although of peasant origin, is the rival of Fitzpiers, a brilliant type of the young country doctor, while the subtle Grace Melbury, daughter of a wood-merchant, finds her counterparts in the humble Marty South, the symbol of an attachment ending only with life, and the disquieting figure of Felicia Charmond, with her adventurous history of coquette and fatal woman. This composition of groups also appears in *Jude the Obscure,* where the hero finds first in Arabella the purely animal creature, representing the will to live, then in Sue the modern daughter of Eve, set free by the intelligence and desirous of escaping from the ritual handed down by the ages, a true apostle of feminism in its dawning stage. These antitheses and oppositions appear no less clearly in *The Return of the Native,* where Clym and Wildeve, Eustacia and Thomasin represent contradictory desires and aspirations. At each turning point of the intrigue we are conscious of the interplay and reactions of these warring forces, the antagonisms of which could be transcribed as upon a working plan. The book is the tragedy of irreconcilable ideals.

In his work, *The Technique of Thomas Hardy* (1922), Mr J. W. Beach conceived the idea of expressing by a species of diagram the relations between the different characters, and in *The Woodlanders* the figure appears in the following form, which expresses the attractive forces at work, allowing one to deduce the respective rivalries:

```
Grace — Fitzpiers — Mrs Charmond
  |
Giles — Melbury    _   _   -   -   -
  |
Marty —    _   -   -
```

A critical examination of many of the couples would always reveal the skilful choice employed by Hardy in bringing incompatible characters to confront one another. The mere fact of the proximity of these beings implies collision, with results that cannot be repaired.

It was no doubt in Nature that Hardy discovered this universal conflict. He beheld it in all its phases, at every stage of life. The episodes of such a conflict make up a drama which knows no end or consummation, set in motion by that Immanent Will, which constitutes the essence of the world.

The forest of plants resembles the forest of human beings. It offers the same spectacle of combats and duels in which the weakest go down and from which the victor himself emerges wounded.

> " Sycamore shoulders oak;
> Bines the slim sapling yoke,
> Ivy-spun halters choke
> Elms stout and tall."[1]

In this work everything holds together. Its impressive architecture recalls the closely interlocked stones of a Cyclopean group.

The spectacle discovered in Nature may be observed in many other domains. Among the conflicts which form the basis of Hardy's novels a place is accorded to the struggle between the past, with its *cortege* of the poetic and the picturesque, and the present, the child of progress, holding no patent of nobility. The Exhibition of 1851 resulted in a veritable invasion of the English countryside by modern

---

[1] *In a Wood, Wessex Poems.* This poem (1896) only summarises a description occurring in *The Woodlanders* (1887).

life. The appearance of the railway was the signal for what really amounted to a revolution in those hamlets where peasants passed their lives beneath their shelter of thatch. *A Laodicean* gives us a picture of this duel of influences of which M. Henry Bordeaux, for instance, has often availed himself. At once ardent and cautious, this combat is staged upon the plane of sentiment between the young Paula Power, daughter of a great railway constructor, heiress of those who are supplanting the age-long owners of property, and Captain de Stancy, a reclaimed rake, now without occupation, heir to a great name. Some aspects of this story have been treated by Hardy quite on the lines of a detective novel, to the detriment of its better parts.

His first glance at life has brought a feeling of pain to the novelist and his spirit at times revolts in the presence of this monstrous universe. First the scenery itself, then the scenes and finally the characters, all are welded together. The tie which holds them so fast runs among them like a conducting thread. To a mechanistic conception of the world the novelist could only reply by a psychology of humanity largely autonomous and existing apart from the Whole. The conflict of the sexes carries on the struggle of the elements, only in another sphere. Both are fought out in the very bosom of Nature, manifesting themselves in the pulsations of life.

Love becomes a force at once objective and subjective. But it belongs more to the sphere of universal phenomena than to that of individual and independent emotions. It illustrates the subordination of the individual to the species, even to the rhythm of a yet vaster system. The Immanent Will which rules the

world guides living creatures by means of the instincts. The clashes and revolts which mark the conflict of the sexes show humanity's effort to reach the
free and wild spaces, where the future of the race
would be secured.

This conception of a struggle carried on upon a
vast scale is no doubt not altogether original. The
mental vigour which it implies recalls other works
and other efforts at generalization. M. René Lalou
makes the following appropriate remarks in his com-
ments upon the comedies of Marivaux : " Everything
takes place as if there were a perpetual struggle going
on between an eternal woman, the image of all
women, and a masculine type, which we all resemble
in a greater or less degree in essential spiritual
characteristics. With inexhaustible patience Marivaux strives to define the phases of this combat and
to distinguish between their various shades. He does
not proclaim the Cartesian theory, but pays it the
most respectful homage, treating it as a psychological
support upon which he can count, as a sure framework, as a guarantee that so many subtle observations will not remain scattered on all hands, but will
be assembled in a permanent unity."[1] Marivaux
saw the forces of egoism narrowly watching one
another. He matched in conflict the beings destined
to love each other. He showed them setting traps for
each other in that struggle wherein both parties alike
assert the will to dominate, which constitute that defence of the ego, where M. René Lalou sees an
affirmation of Cartesianism.

In Marivaux we see brilliant passes made with foils,

[1] René Lalou. *Défense de l'Homme (De Descartes à Proust)*
Kra.

from which the buttons are not removed. The combatants emerge without a scratch. In Hardy, too, the conflict of the sexes aims at the abolition of the human categories in the interests of a general law. But the struggle develops in time with a cruel rhythm. There are those who fall; there are bleeding bodies.

Let us take a general survey of the representation of these conflicts, wherein impelled by their blind instincts, the two creatures assail one another in the effort to discover which shall gain the upper hand and give law to the vanquished. Everywhere at the same time the two show the same obstinate will to live and the same need for domination. Alternately pursuer and pursued, they have recourse to the wonderful strategy suggested by the instincts, an expression of the most intense will to live. In a spirit of fierce competition, the creatures surrender themselves to bitter strife, in order to perpetuate the race, their efforts often ending in merely providing an unappeasable Moloch with new and innocent victims. The spectacle before one is the terrible spectacle of energies poured forth in pure waste. For what scanty advantage are they expended? In Hardy's work the child is an incident rather than an end in itself. Except for poor Tess's offspring so speedily carried off and Jude's children all doomed to die, the child plays no role in *Wessex Novels* and *Poems*.

Our task will be to discover affinities among so many aspects of violence.

May it not be said that it was Hardy's aim to write the history of humanity in love, disengaging the eternal forces from their immediate context? He examines these ephemeral heroes " sub specie aeternitatis " amid the conflicts through which he conducts them. The mighty monotony of all destinies expresses a law of unity.

" The lives of Marty and Giles seemed completely isolated and self-contained in the grey of the morning, yet were part of the pattern in the great web of human doings from the White Sea to Cape Horn."[1]

Such is indeed the thought of Thomas Hardy, deeply imbued with the idea of that *All-pervading Cause*, of the unity which gives to his work itself that note of *monotony*, to which the sensitive feeling of a Marcel Proust[2] has paid the tribute of a great æsthetic thinker, speaking from the fulness of his knowledge of what conditions a work of art.

---

1 " *The Woodlanders*." The text of this quotation differs from that of the Macmillan edition of 1919, vol. VIII, p. 23 of the *Wessex Novels*, but we preferred it for reasons of explicitness.
2 Marcel Proust, *La Prisonnière*, pp. 235-237, T II.

CHAPTER V

PASSION AND NECESSITY

" Who ever lov'd, that lov'd not at first sight? "
As You Like It, Act III, Scene V.

" Go, ask his name :—if he be married,
My grave is like to be my wedding bed."
Romeo and Juliet, Act I, Scene V.

ONE naturally looks for a definition of the sentiment of love in the work of a writer who makes it the rallying point for everything that has life.

Hardy finds his spokesman in the doctor, Edred Fitzpiers, in the *The Woodlanders*. Nourished on German metaphysics, the young doctor sees in love a subjective sentiment, the very essence of man according to Spinoza's definition, an idea of joy projected against the screen provided by a human being :

" Human love is a subjective thing—the essence itself of man as that great thinker Spinoza says— ' ipsa hominis essentia '—it is joy accompanied by an idea which we project against any suitable object in the light of our vision, just as the rainbow iris is projected against an oak, ash, or elm tree indifferently."[1]

1 *The Woodlanders.* Chapter XVI.

This idea is throughout valuable as a counterpoise to those manifestations of love, which seem to be encroached upon by the fleshly element supporting them and by all its reactions.

Love does not remain a mere latent force hidden away within the confines of potentiality. It is a will which desires to express itself and must, therefore, project itself against every being within its reach, like the image which projects itself against the screen offered to it, or to preserve Hardy's expression with greater fidelity, like the rainbow which bestows its colours indifferently upon the oak, ash or elm tree.

This will which acts like a spring, unchanging and hidden from the world, doubtless constituting the thing in itself, manifests itself in that invincible need for love inherent in living things.

Thus in love the Immanent Will wields greater power than the spiritual forces.

This purely external projection appears in the *The Well-Beloved*, where Pierston is, as will be seen, always in quest of an imaginary chimera, a very sylphid of his dreams, the wandering incarnation of his need for love. But, in this case, the hero is perhaps artificial, and the author has undoubtedly allowed himself relaxation. In *The Return of the Native* occur other examples confirming the interpretation suggested here. In its pages the writer depicts with great power and wealth of detail two inhabitants of the fatal heath, Clym who adores it, and Eustacia who detests it. Both are to become in their love the victims of a process of crystallization, to employ Stendhal's language. The young woman comes unconsciously to love the being who is destined to occupy the void within her soul, while Clym

goes forth to find the companion who should become
the help-meet he seeks in his projects of study and
instruction. The preparation is, therefore, ideal,
solitary, and imaginative. If the road is different
from that so often travelled, the end of the journey
is the same as in all other cases. It is in a sudden
swift embrace, a trifle disconcerting in its quickness,
that the two chief characters conclude the first stage
of their journey.

One might repeat Hardy's metaphor from *The
Woodlanders* of the two beings " charged with
emotive fluid like a Leyden jar with electric, for want
of some conductor at hand to disperse it."

In the *Poems of the Past and the Present* Hardy
once more took up this theme of the purely ideal
projection against a screen not always worthy of the
sentiment expressed.

> " The sprite resumed; ' Thou hast transferred
>   To her dull form awhile
> My beauty, fame, and deed and word,
>   My gestures and my smile.' "[1]

Jude offers the example least open to discussion
of the psychical structure upon which love rests;
" His idea of her was the thing of most consequence,
not Arabella herself. . . .[2]

From the actual essence of the sentiment we must
now pass to its more ordinary manifestations.

The German philosopher to whom Hardy was most
closely related (for he did not, as has been wrongly
contended, remain outside of and apart from all
cultural influence), Schopenhauer, said that if one
would write the metaphysics of love, he must

1 *The Well-Beloved. Poems of the Past and the Present.*
2 *Jude the Obscure.* p. 55.

assuredly begin by studying its physics. In the same way Hardy seems to reach his final conception only after having depicted all foregoing and concomitant phenomena.

It results from this that a complete understanding of the pair demands that one should follow in detail throughout all these works the process of formation of the amorous sentiment and group together a certain number of traits which will reveal the principal themes of the variations.

But if love does indeed pre-exist in its object and, therefore, owes its origin to a kind of parthenogenesis, the mere spatial condition of immediate contiguity is not enough to cause it to appear. Human beings are not infinitely interchangeable; that must never be supposed. The necessity only exists, if the chosen types are actually face to face. Change the actors, and you will no longer observe the phenomenon in its full perfection. The categorical imperative which they obey depends upon very definite factors.

The encounter of Jude and Arabella appears before us as a prototype. It is decisive. " . . . There was a momentary flash of intelligence, a dumb announcement of affinity *in posse* between herself and him."

Two forces at once friendly and hostile, have just recognised one another in a sudden flash of lightning. This gleam of light has revealed to both that they must unite within the structure of the pair. The desires lurking within the flesh of each have been divined, their precocious affinity is purely instinctive.

" I want him to have me, to marry me," Arabella at once declares with the female animal's brutal

sincerity, and Jude, a novice in the intellectual field,
who has not learned how to " repress his sexuality
through the medium of the brain," is made to offer
himself up defenceless to the coarse wiles of this
woman's vulgar sensuality. In describing what
draws Jude towards Arabella, Hardy shows how the
individual's freedom of will has disappeared, sucked
down into the shifting sands of desire, and he describes the force which drives him towards this
woman with the words, " as a violent schoolmaster
a schoolboy he has seized."[1]

Later in the same novel, the partial intellectualism
of Jude and Sue is not so artificial as to mar the profound simplicity of the problem which haunts the
whole book. Their intellectualism hardly suffices to
confer upon it a form at once more sharply outlined
and more social, for the subject-matter continues
always sober and passionately human, while yet
preserving a freedom, a force and a frankness, recalling the liberating impulse of the *Kreutzer Sonata*.
No doubt the first meeting between Jude and Sue
lacks the note of sensuality that marked the moment
when he first pressed Arabella's hand. Yet this
idyll, in which the spirit is assigned a greater rôle
than the flesh, none the less confronts us with the
problem of the human pair. At first Jude beheld in
Sue " liquid untranslatable eyes, which combined
. . . keenness with tenderness, and mystery with
both. . . ." And the reaction was not slow in coming.
Jude felt the whole wealth of poetry stored within
him streaming towards her. But he was soon to long
that the companion of his spirit should become the
comrade of his flesh.

1 *Jude the Obscure.* Part I, Chapter VII.

These first observations show why Hardy chose his principal characters from among those living a rustic life. The protagonists in his dramas are often peasants brought up in close contact with nature. When he mingles with them a few intellectuals, lawyers, clergymen, or architects like himself, these intruders seem a little lost in the surroundings of the land. The author, in fact, understood that he must seek for the most sincere expressions of love from among simple people, peasants, from among that multitude of beings who, according to the powerful expression of Anatole France, are vowed to the "august and rugged task of winning their daily bread, who are the repositories of the true morality, of the real virtues of an entire people." It is, therefore, among these peasants living in close and unbroken contact with the realities of heaven and earth that love will remain in the full amplitude of its extent, elemental, the primary motive force.[1] Desirous of becoming acquainted with man as he is, divested of all his artificial attributes, the novelist hardly ever leaves the Wessex which he knows so well. In Wessex he studies not indeed society itself, but the cell out of which it is formed, the human pair, the basis of human activities and the source of their continued existence. The relations between the sexes always constitute the main problem in his work, and he sets out to show us the working of in-

---

[1] An essay of Hardy's, which appeared in 1888, contains these very explicit words : " The conduct of the upper classes is screened by conventions and thus the real character is not easily seen; if it is seen, it must be portrayed subjectively, whereas in the lower walks conduct is a direct expression of the inner life; and thus character can be easily portrayed through. In one case the author's word has to be taken as to the nerves and muscles of his figures; in the other they can be seen."

stinct and sexual attraction in the formation of these
pairs.

As the writer loves to demonstrate, it is Nature's
scheme to bring two human beings to the point at
which it seems that an irresistible attraction must
soon draw them towards one another.

A passage occurs in *Tess* expressing this belief in
a ruthless necessity. The metaphors employed are
themselves irrefutable proofs of it. " All the mean-
while, they were converging under an irresistible law,
as surely as two streams in one vale." " He was
driven towards her by every impulse of his heart."
But the exact significance of these indications has
yet to grow in power and definiteness. Thus for a
long time Angel and Tess confront one another pain-
fully like two forces which passion has only succeeded
in opposing one to the other. Were it not for the
fear of exaggerating the comparisons, one might
even say that they studied one another, standing on
the brink of passion, somewhat as two wild animals
watch each other, before tearing one another to
pieces. At last comes the moment when the woman's
flesh speaks too eloquently to the son of parson Clare,
and when there remains but one possibility, that of
a chaste embrace, a climax long prepared and long
awaited, like the fall of an overripe fruit, consequent
upon the slightest breath of wind. And this rapid
process of evolution from reserve to surrender runs
its course like some phenomenon of attraction
governed by a law of physics. Once more; the
metaphor used by Hardy to put the final touches
upon the descriptions of this first kiss leaves no room
for doubt as to how he must have regarded the
phenomenon : " Nobody had beheld the gravitation

of the two into one," he wrote. His style is in the last degree significant upon this point. To pass by without studying it can only result in failure to perceive the astronomic character which the novelist desired to impose upon these phenomena of attraction. In *The Hand of Ethelberta* he says of the heroine and Julian, "nothing less than Atlantean force could overpower their natural gravitation towards each other." The author's very loyalty to these comparisons bathes his vision of the pair in an astral light. *The Return of the Native* the honeymoon of Clym and Eustacia is presented in the following terms : "They were like those double stars which revolve round each other, and from a distance appear to be one."[1] These expressions, therefore, do not result from pure chance. They reflect what is almost a deliberately doctrinaire attitude towards the phenomenon.

But let us return to our milkmaid, Tess. Her first surrender is followed by a reaction. She makes a sincere and perfectly natural effort to recover herself. What gifts will marred virginity shower upon the soft Angel Clare ? What delicate attitudes are here depicted with a freshness and emotion all aglow ! But the contest is resumed with all the greater ardour between the enamoured Angel and the milkmaid, determined in her virtuous modesty not to deceive the lover who believes her to be pure. What, then, can love do but sweep her along in its full tide ? If there is reserve and modesty in Tess, there is also absolute submission to the great law of love, the all-ruler in that solitary farm amid the nerve-ridden

[1] *The Return of the Native. The closed door.* I.

infection which kindles the same desires in all the young women. " I can't bear anybody to have him, but me," cries Tess in words that are forerunners of those uttered by Arabella, when she meets Jude.

There are indeed many other points of resemblance which compel a comparison between the stories of Tess and Jude, both of them creatures of adversity. The two books tell the story of their fall, and after the defiling touch from the hand of Alec the love of Angel and Tess knows the same purity as that felt by Sue and Jude after the abnormal contact with Arabella. It blooms forth with the same freshness and Tess remains true to the idea of her unworthiness, just as Sue struggles to restore her faith in the first husband whom she did not love. The sensitive natures of the two women have the same need for sincerity, but after what a series of reverses. For in Hardy's work the woman who has been wounded by deception and cruelty in her first love seeks refuge in silence, in recoiling upon herself; and then comes the reaction of surrender to the first impression of a new affection. Finally the woman devours the evil which preys upon her, absorbing it into the depths of her being. Thereafter she seems to be born anew to life. Green shoots spring from the stock. She is stricken dumb by an unexpected happiness; and when the unconquerable need for sincerity manifests itself, the catastrophe is inevitable, the bitter fruit of a late and necessary avowal.[1] Is not this to some extent the story of that Elfride whom we have already met, who pays with her happiness for making confession of her first love ?[2] In these pages the

1 See note on Freud and Hardy. p. 191.
2 See Chapter IV, " The Conflict of the Sexes."

principal characters have a kind of fore-knowledge of their own destinies. Before crossing the Rubicon of avowal, before the dice are cast, they hesitate and finally shrink back because they are certain to lose everything.

It is not only between the stories of Tess and Jude that parallels exist.

Arriving at a general rule, without perhaps seeking it, Hardy discovers identically similar facts at every step. In his books the destinies often pursue paths in common or run parallel to one another, or suddenly meet at unexpected cross-roads.

Moreover the human pair is frequently subjected to ill-usage by the same freaks of fortune. Encased within the breasts which shelter them, the hearts of these peasants and peasant-women beat with some rapidity. But the beats are set going by the same cause, and so true is this that the multiplicity of aspects and of vicissitudes without end, that present themselves throughout these volumes, cannot mask from us the existence of a real and deeply-seated unity. It is, indeed, this unity which has led to the conception of this book which, without it, could never have come into being. In all ranks of society the same passion produces results, if not exactly alike, at least very similar to one another. Whether it is the farmer Boldwood in *Far from the Madding Crowd* or Dick Dewy in *Under the Greenwood Tree*, the charm cast by love upon their lives gives rise to a state of mind in each case of the same order.

A cruel and tormenting sentiment in Hardy, as in Racine, love appears in the guise of a despot. Both achieve the creation of types. Arabella and Sue are incarnations in the same sense as Phèdre and Roxane.

Investing his figures with their full value as characters from the earliest chapters, the novelist establishes a solid basis upon which to build. When he seeks to portray them, he surprises them as they are in their everyday life, without tearing them from their daily task. Thus we never behold them set upon a pedestal of convention. But it is only on the very eve of love that the writer brings them together, taking up his position for a deliberate methodical observation. Soon he sees his characters hurled against one another with a coefficient of acceleration corresponding to his own philosophical and aesthetic dynamism.

The author composes his tragedy much as a historical painter lays the paint upon the great canvas of a battle-scene (for with Hardy it is always the battle of the sexes). In one corner he indicates the preparations, and on the horizon he depicts the effects. The contest occupies the centre of the canvas. To construct this synthesis he unites these three phases like the links of an unbroken chain. This chain, which confers all their unity upon his love-scenes, without taking from them a whit of their complexity, is no other than the chain of passion. Harsh necessity is forged amid the iron links of which it is formed.

Suddenness, finality and fatalism endow the love-story with their own virtue of dramatic intensity and fierce and rapid interest. They confer a birth-mark upon the human creatures, a guise by which we may know them for Hardy's characters.

Yet blind though they are, these forces are none the less active in an atmosphere, which is often not without its own softness. And puissant though they continue, they still do not stifle a certain caressing superfluity, from which a morning's ecstasy may be born.

It is thus that the corners and the roughness of his work are often smoothed beneath a down of silky sheen. The nicest and least perceptible distinctions did not escape this observer, who was at the same time a philosopher. In the chromatic scale of an ever-growing sentiment each ascendant degree is noted; the distance between all the tones is measured; the hesitations, the weaknesses, the timidities, and the appoggiaturas before certain notes all are recorded.

Hardy is quite at ease in this ineffable region. In the midst of these seductions he finds delight in their least decisive moments. The lanes of the Wessex villages are his gardens of love, but he has inhaled all their perfumes at the most various hours. He has experienced to the full the sweetness that hovers about the brutal force which is called love, and knows what graceful and charming surrenders accompany the seizure of a heart.

Passion and necessity ravage the heart of Grace Melbury,[1] but even in their merciless embrace she continues to live uncertain and wavering as a climbing plant, a fragile being poised in the valleys of Hintock.

In a book which even now retains an astonishing freshness, Sénancour has shown by what processes attraction in its most rugged shapes evolves towards a more docile form: " It cannot be doubted that in several species Nature herself, by prompting the male to an urgent demand for pleasure, suggests to the female the idea of evading the laws for a moment,

1 *The Woodlanders.*

in order to yield to them after her own manner. But the free activity which distinguishes man adds to these various movements sentiments, the delicacy of which may degenerate into singular pretentions. The abrupt attack of the one sex and the simple resistance of the other have been transformed into a vast number of methods of attack and resistance. *Amour-propre* wages a defensive, too often an offensive warfare full of skill, subtlety, and falseness."[1]

[1] De l'amour selon les lois primordiales et selon les convenances des sociétés modernes (1806).

CHAPTER VI

THE MYSTERY OF ATTRACTIONS

" It's a deep mystery—the way the heart of man turns to one woman out of all the rest he's seen in the world . . . ."

GEORGE ELIOT, *Adam Bede*, Chap. III, Book I.

" Do you know what is to love and be loved ? Do you know—not by hearsay merely, but by experience —this absorption of one human being in another, the one man in the one woman, the one woman in the one man ?

LUCAS MALET, *The Wages of Sin*, 1891.

HAVING described the nature of love as it appears in Hardy's works and having made the acquaintance of several of his characters, who have become martyrs for love, the next step is to approach the study of the phenomena and of their contents—in short, to analyse them. If love becomes a function of the affinities which call it into action, if, in fact, the lovers " magnetize " one another, there lies before us a region which we must now explore. It is the region of unconquerable attraction, the existence of which we have already set on record in the course of the previous chapter.

In those works where Hardy's conception of love has not yet shewn all the cruelty of its countenance the mysterious nature of sexual attractions is none the less insisted upon. Feminine or masculine in origin, they produce the same irrevocable effects.

It is the inexorable and disquieting character of the charm that supplies the writer with the whole of his themes. Hardy would seem to depict the relations between man and woman as apparently governed by frivolous causes, but in reality he shews that they are determined by the obscure forces springing from the instincts and even from a power yet more essential to the world. We must not be deceived by the suddenness and caprice with which certain sentimental emotions seem to burst into flower, even when their appearance threatens to set all reason at defiance. The unions which he outlines are not thereby rendered futile. Rather it is that there will be a note of precariousness, which will justify all the shafts aimed by destiny. Misfortune will arrive as vengeance and ransom for the reason which has been betrayed. Thus the coupling of Jude and Arabella (for there is no other word to characterize this union) contains the germ of all the vicissitudes of their short married life.

With Hardy's characters love in its opening stages commonly reveals itself in the form of a decree of destiny which gives rise to some fixed idea. It is in reality the appeal of sex, the language of the male or the female that we hear sometimes employing words of unusual ingenuousness. " I must have him, I can't do without him. He is the sort of man I long for. I shall go mad if I can't give myself to him altogether. I felt I should when I first saw him."[1]

As Proudhon said, " Love, alike whether we consider it as the effect of the power of generation, or whether we relate it to the ideal, is entirely withdrawn from the will of the individual who feels it. It is born spontaneously, undesignedly and fatally. It appears without our knowing it and in our despite."

As the subject of his special choice Hardy reserves the keenest of his powers for depicting the dawn of the amorous sentiment. From their very nature the earliest impressions felt always reveal emotions which particularly affect certain sides of the sensibility. In proof of this let us give the following example : Saint-Cleeve and Viviette (*Two on a Tower*) meet for the first time and the novelist at once notes what he describes as " a reciprocity of influence . . . making itself apparent in the faces of each."

He discovers the mysterious interchange of two sensibilities, confronting one another for the first time, but acting upon one another and thereby modifying one another with the same rigorous necessity as if they were two chemical bodies brought together.

---

1 *Jude the Obscure.* This first encounter between Arabella and Jude will remain famous in the annals of the English novel. The very crudeness with which it is recounted makes it one of Hardy's finest discoveries of its special kind. Lost in his dreams of study, Jude returns to the old aunt who has adopted him. He moves indifferent to the world's clamour. Suddenly he receives something in the face. What is it? The sexual organ of a boar which a girl with fine black eyes, busy at some task on the other side of the river, has thrown at him as a kind of challenge. And this trivial action on the part of a girl, who wishes to tantalise him, at once interrupts his train of thought and decides the whole course of his life.

If the phrase be allowed, the charm of a human being acts in a material manner. The effect that is felt is not merely that of the moral disturbance which results. With Hardy there appears what is almost an anguish of the flesh, which the writer describes as " the unvoiced call of woman to man." Men and women frequently feel the effects of the same inexplicable and instantaneous attraction, followed by the same haunting sensation. Tolstoy, too, gazed deep into this mystery of the flesh. He confesses it in his *Kreutzer Sonata*, written in 1889. " The noblest and the most poetic form of love, as we term it, depends not upon moral qualities, but upon physical intimacy . . . ." To be exact one should perhaps write " physical pre-intimacy."

The actual physical approach of certain persons gives rise to disquieting reactions, the laws of which Schopenhauer has described by analogy in the following terms : " Two lovers must neutralise one another like the acids and alkalis in neutral salts." The author of *Two on a Tower* thus expresses the element of rigour and brutality in the suddenness with which love reveals itself : " The alchemy which thus transmuted an abstracted astronomer into an eager lover . . . may almost be described as working its change in one short night."[1]

To accept such opinions it is to sink deeply into that organic fatalism with which Hardy seems to

---

[1] When Captain de Stancy (A Laodicean) catches sight of the young Paula on her trapeze, his demoniacal son at once observes the effects which might be looked for in that amateur of the fair sex : " A fermentation is beginning in him. . . a purely chemical process, and when it is complete, he will probably be clear and fiery and sparkling, and quite another man than the good, weak, and easy fellow that he was." Book II, Chapter VII.

have stamped all the episodes where sexuality predominates.

The uneasiness which seizes upon man and woman alike, when they find themselves in the presence of the chosen one, reappears in almost every novel with a dogmatic regularity of recurrence.

Face to face with the being with whom she feels the greatest measure of affinity a woman with so much command of her heart and nerves as Ethelberta is conscious of an overwhelming sense of disquiet against which she can effect nothing, disquiet amid which the flesh declares itself in terms that may not be gainsaid.

" At hearing him speak all the delicate activities in the young lady's person stood still : she stopped like a clock. When she could again fence with the perception which had caused all this, she breathed."[1] Yet Ethelberta is predominantly a creature who struggles to withdraw herself from the influence of all reflexes. But here it is enough to recognise that voice which echoes so deeply within her for her to become conscious of that impression of shock and of a secret sense of subordination to another.

A sentiment which thus speaks in terms of emotive forces—stoppages of the heart-beats, blushing or growing pale—imposes at certain moments a passive obedience to the feelings now set free from all control. The individual becomes a mere serf. This submission implies other factors besides reason, besides even free will. It rather displays the influence of certain waves which would seem to emanate from the animal substance and would act only upon

1 *The Hand of Ethelberta.*

organisms capable of receiving them in virtue of some unknown synchronism.

One is brought back to the ever just, if less complex phrase in the *Caractères*:

"Love is born suddenly without any reflection; it is born of temperament or weakness: a flash of beauty catches us and determines our course."[1]

Born of purely physical contingencies, the lot of love must necessarily be hazardous. Its destiny must continue as uncertain as its earliest hours, themselves determined by the promptings of sex. Above all things love will continue to be a condition dominated by passion which, like the sea, will know the wrath of the tempest, the tidal waves, and the surging of the under-current breaking amid the tumult of the storm.

Let us examine the points of detail as presented by Hardy in his meticulous observations of the early stages of love.

Under the Greenwood Tree is a country-life fantasy, wherein we are made acquainted with the attitude of Dick Dewy. The young minstrel who goes the rounds at Christmas has just beheld the fascinating Fancy Day, the village schoolmistress. "Opposite the window, leaning motionless against a beech-tree, was the lost man, his head thrown back, his eyes fixed upon the illuminated lattice." Later on the author returns to the first effects of passion, as it begins to act upon him who has lately become a lover. "Dick's slumbers, through the three or four hours remaining for rest, were disturbed and slight; an exhaustive variation upon the incidents that had passed that night in connection with the

1 La Bruyère, *Caractères*, Du Cœur.

school window, going on in his brain every moment of the time."

Here love shews itself as the result of a physiological shock. Hardy's heroes are all of them subject to this brutal incursion of a sentiment which may involve the whole future of a life.

Eustacia[1] tells us that it was enough for her to see a hussar officer riding down the street to fall madly in love with him. And yet she does not know the man personally.

The case of farmer Boldwood is extremely instructive. It represents a fully mature man who has lived in utter ignorance of women and who suddenly awakens, blinded by an unexpected flash of light.

Bathsheba has noticed that at the corn-market Boldwood pays her no attention. His indifference rouses her. She sends him a playful valentine. It was like a scented rose flung in the face of the forty-year-old man, and the gesture of impertinent coquetry unchains a passion which knows no limits. Making its appearance at the very noontide of life, passion becomes with this man a fire which consumes the whole of his being. A frenzied monomania seizes upon his soul and overpowers his will.

Let us dwell upon the effects of the terrible thing that closes vault-like about his head, making the farmer a kind of somnambulist, losing himself more and more in the maze of his fixed idea. Listen to this conversation with Gabriel Oak. The avowal of the negligent ways into which Boldwood has fallen shews the gravity of his disorder:

" Your ricks are all covered before this time ? "

" No."

1 *The Return of the Native.*

" At any rate the large ones upon the stone staddles ? "

" They are not."

" Them under the hedge ? "

" No, I forgot to tell the thatcher to set about it."

" Nor the little one by the stile ? "

" Nor the little one by the stile. I overlooked the ricks this year."

Such is the aspect of Boldwood in *Far From the Madding Crowd.* Love gnaws at him like an internal disease, a canker of the flesh and brain. On one page he is seen approaching on horseback, like some horseman in the Vision of the Apocalypse. Hardy has outlined him for us as in an etching. Is it not like the spectre of grief itself looming up in the chilly air of the early morning? " The want of colour in his well defined face, the enlarged appearance of the veins in the forehead and the temples, and the sharper outlines about his mouth . . . ." tell of the pangs and ravages of passion.

Love, then, has all the characteristics of a sudden revelation. It causes a kind of fissure in ordinary everyday life. What we see most frequently asserted is the ascendancy which the man exercises at first sight over the woman who is soon to become subject to his law. In *The Romantic Adventures of a Milkmaid* there occur these very significant lines : " He was like a magician to me. I think he was one . . . . He could move me as a loadstone moves a speck of steel." Hardy explained this strange power of fascination in terms of greater exactness in the following phrase : " Margery always declared that there seemed some power in the stranger that was more than human, something magical and compulsory, when he seized her . . . ." Other examples show even better how closely Hardy's heroines resemble one another. With slight differences of character, they are all daughters of the same Eve by right of love's reactions upon them, until at length they become the victims of a veritable hallucination.

The following is what one reads in one of the stories in *Life's Little Ironies*, " The Fiddler of the Reels " : " The next evidences of his influence upon her were singular enough and it would require a neurologist to fully explain them. . . . Without a moment's warning . . . she would start from her seat in the chimney corner, as if she had received a galvanic shock, and spring convulsively towards the ceiling." And the whole cause of this strange conduct is the fiddler's twanging string. There are indeed numerous scenes of seduction in which music plays its part in the final capture of a spirit. This observation brings us back to a more lively chapter in another book, where Tess, only recently come to the farm of Talbothays, hears the quavering tones of the harp of Angel Clare, which drowns her in a kind of beatitude. This whole series of data operate to emphasise the importance of all the emotional impressions in the formation of the sentiment of love. In *Desperate Remedies*, an early book, we also see the charm of music at work. Observe this young woman, listening to an organist : " New impulses of thought came with new harmonies and entered into her with gnawing thrill."

In conjunction with this influence of music allusion might be made to the influence of dancing. Everything that engages the feelings upon smiling slopes

and in winding ways unlooked for turns life aside from
its practical courses and creates a readiness to yield
to sentimental thoughts. Eustacia finds Wildeve at a
country ball and, rocked in the arms of this man,
she lives again through her dreams as a young girl
for whom marriage has meant sacrifice. And Margery, the milkmaid, when she waltzes with the baron ?
And Fancy Day with Dick Dewy as her cavalier,
has not the process of conquest already begun ?[1]
Dancing and music are two accomplices who contrive
the downfall of many.

The fiddler knows this well :

> " There's many a heart now mangled,
>   And waiting its time to go,
>   Whose tendrils were first entangled
>   By my sweet viol and bow."[2]

Yet in the work of seduction dancing and music
are mere accessories, no more.

Somewhere Hardy had noted that man loves with
his eyes, woman through her sense of hearing. In
this way he justifies the hold that music acquires.
But curious though it be, this remark has no absolute value. The writer keeps contradicting himself
regarding the point throughout the book, in which the
impulse in particular to show the decisive role played
by masculine beauty in the formation of the sentiment seems overwhelmingly strong. In *Desperate
Remedies* we read these lines : " She was interested
in him and and his marvellous beauty, as she might
have been in some fascinating panther or leopard."
This influence of masculine beauty recurs in the

---

1 *Under the Greenwood Tree.* Chap. VIII.
2 *The Fiddler. Time's Laughingstocks.*

manner of a " leit-motiv," and each time, in the pages
devoted to love's opening phases, it proclaims the
preeminence of all the impressions felt by Hardy's
characters as physical sensations. In *A Pair of Blue
Eyes* Elfride surrenders to love like Miranda at the
appearance of Ferdinand, but the miracle has been
accomplished by the young man's face : " . . . . The
ascendancy over her that his face and not his parts
had acquired for him."

Going beyond the idea of this solitary æsthetic
influence, Hardy finds a satisfaction in insisting upon
the sentiment of masculine superiority and of the
ascendancy which it enjoys. " He seemed to be her
ruler rather than her equal."[1] he writes of one of his
heroes. Thus the exquisite Grace Melbury allows
herself to be fascinated by the strange young doctor,
Fitzpiers.[2] Favoured by a somewhat romantic noc-
turnal adventure, behold her all of a sudden in the
doctor's arms, and she finds in the suddenness of the
embrace the revelation of a force, to the domination
of which she must now submit. She feels herself completely mastered from the very outset and some
moments must pass before she can emerge from her
confusion. She is astonished at the road over which
she has unwittingly travelled, when still giddy and
trembling she leaves the doctor, her cheeks all aflame.
A little later Hardy uses the word " intoxication "
to describe the way in which the charm of Fitzpiers,
the seductive libertine, has acted upon the young girl.
There is then in this mysterious fatality which for
ever links together the existences of two human beings
by the revelation of unknown affinities, suddenly ap-

1 *The Woodlanders.*
2 *The Woodlanders*

pearing by the mere exchange of a look, the whole genesis of the sentiment of love as conceived by Hardy, with the predominance of the most highly characterized affective elements.

Let us consider another typical illustration. It is the case of Cytherea Graye, the heroine of *Desperate Remedies*, and one of the earliest born among Hardy's girls, since this was the first novel which he published. Here we have first of all a young girl admirably prepared for the adventures of love along the lines laid down by Hardy. Her brother by his flattering description of Springrove has created in her what really amounts to a condition of sentimental receptivity. Her heredity has also predestined Cytherea to an adventure of this kind. For her father has been the victim of one of those sudden and irresistible loves, the spectacle of which inspired the ancients in their imaginings of love-philtres and mysterious potions. How then escape from such a convergence of influences? They immediately create a magnetic field wherein all the potential affinities reveal themselves. A chance encounter places the girl in the presence of Springrove. The fluid acts immediately. As soon as it begins to radiate, it creates a perfect intimacy between these souls which at once imagine themselves to be united for the whole of life. The powers of attraction reach their most complete expression in woman, the more sensitive creature, the vessel in the crystals of which the emotions find their longest refraction. Sometimes they are only the immediate echo of the beauty of the male, of his ascendancy or of the even more disquieting seduction practised by intellectual superiority. Lady Viviette Constantine in *Two on a Tower*

is conscious of her admiration for the young and
learned Swithin who dwells exclusively within the
realm of speculation, and Hardy with the sure touch
of an observer accustomed to discover women's most
secret reactions notes that a " warmer wave of her
warm temperament glowed visibly through her."
Viviette looks upon Swithin's parted lips which seem
already to converse with infinite space. The further
she feels them to be from her, the more actively sensual emotions stir within her. She suddenly finds
herself grown younger by " ten summers " and this
transfiguration finally prepares her for the love which
discovers a favourable soil in this abandoned wife,
who can neither direct nor expand the energies of her
sentimentality. But if these heroines sometimes
strive to contend against the fatal attractions which
must hold them in thrall, they should also be able
to thwart events. For events suddenly become the
accomplices of the disorders of their hearts and press
forward to bestow their sanction upon the invitation
held out by nature.

One Friday evening Lady Constantine enters the
dimly lighted church. She kneels down before the
text of the Ten Commandments and strives to tear
out from her heart all the fibres which stretch towards
Saint Cleeve. And then, at the very moment when
she struggles to abandon herself completely to everything that urges her to banish dreams of love from
her thoughts, fate accords her a revelation most propitious to the stirrings of her heart. The vicar passes
close to her. He has just learned of the death of
Viviette's husband far away in Africa. He tells her
of it. May not, then, this Balzacian heroine, enslaved
to the demon of desire, conclude that she is from now

onward set free, that she may love without fear of guilt ?[1] Thus Hardy links events themselves in intimate association with the formation of the pair. We must return later to discuss in greater detail this topic of external influences.[2] Every union becomes in this way dependent upon chance encounters, upon chance in general. It continues subject to the sway of contingencies in no way different from those that have called it into being. These elements, brought into conjunction with one another, gradually group themselves to form—if we may here use the language of philosophy—that representation of the human pair which constitutes one of the loftiest characteristics of Hardy's work. Thus there is a strict correspondence between a great mass of facts and a body of views regarding the relations between man and woman.

The importance which Hardy assigned to the question of the sexes cannot, therefore, be interpreted as a purely fortuitous manifestation. At that time the air was saturated with a certain number of ideas which appear in Hardy's work like a kind of emanation. In 1871 appeared Darwin's book, *The Descent of Man and Selection in Relation to Sex.*

According to the great naturalist, in addition to Natural Selection we have Sexual Selection which completes the former. Thus is revealed the part played by sex in the development and improvement of the species. The superiority of certain individuals of the same sex and species becomes manifest at the moment of procreation. The strongest and most

---

1 *Two on a Tower.* Chap. IX.
2 See Chapter IX. " The Human Pair Amid the Storm of Circumstance."

beautiful males are chosen. Violence is often responsible for handing over the female to the sturdiest among the males, but Darwin adds that there also exists, on the other hand, in the female a power of discrimination which reveals a sense of beauty. For, in many of the cases observed, the female is free to choose between several males. We are condemned by our ignorance to fail in any attempt to discover all the motive forces governing this selection, in their application to several points. According to Darwin's view the instinct which directs the choice is not a blind force, acting without any knowledge of its bearings. He believed that he could distinguish in this instinct the most useful servant of the race. Why should this idea not reappear on the human plane when analogous phenomena are being studied ? It seems reasonable that with his naturalist's conception of love Hardy may have remembered Darwin, or that, directed by convergent influences, the writer's thoughts may, in virtue of their predominantly instinctive character, have approached the outlook of the theorist of evolution. With Hardy, indeed, the dominant impression is that of a man and woman striving to match one another in conformity with the higher ends of the species. In spite of all psychological reactions which confer a more complex character upon the formation of the pair, it is always the mighty voice of the race that we hear resounding through so many sorrowful echoes.

This influence of Darwin harmonises admirably with the principles enunciated by Schopenhauer in the *Metaphysics of Love*.

Some of Hardy's principal ideas regarding sexual

love appear in that brief essay. The novelist has
provided rugged, concrete examples for the often
over rigid and summary thesis of the philosopher.
In his work the boutade of the German takes on the
substance of the whole, in which it is merged and
assimilated.

For Schopenhauer, too, love has no other root but
instinct. Instinct it is that prescribes possession, and
behind its sensual mask lies hidden the need to perpetuate the species. Thus the will to live pursues
human beings without their being consciously aware
of it. In order that this purpose of procreation may
be perfectly realised, it is once more necessary, as
with Darwin, that a given type of man should be
united with a given type of woman. In this process
of mutual choice instinct supplants every other
guide, because instinct alone is capable of offering
violence to reasoned or interested preferences. Under
the discipline of instinct man forgets the conventions
and some of his own egoism and aspirations. Every
being is disposed to love, without indeed any aware-
ness of this disposition, with a view to reproduction.
To adopt the phrase of Chamfort: " By separating
us from our reason Nature increases the strength of
her own empire over us." Each seeks in his partner
for those qualities most lacking in himself, in order
to create a descendant true to the character of the
race whose survival is at stake. Almost in spite of
themselves, the lovers defer to a regard for equilibrium. It may be observed that unions of contrasted
types secure in the descendants an average of qualities by attenuating and correcting deficiencies or
excesses. The genius of the species acts like an experienced stage-manager, whose political designs

remain hidden from the eyes of the actors. *Contraria contrariis curantur.*

The interplay of attractions that we have been contemplating is thus for Hardy merely the interplay of the suggestions of the species. The individuals conscious of it are subordinate to the instincts dominated by the race. Brutal, sudden and impulsive, the attractions which we have analysed establish a merciless determinism. The formation of every pair, therefore, takes place in subordination to this initial law and the characters which it implies are thus fixed from the very outset in a high relief, wherein every letter harbours not a little menace in its shadow.

A lesson of intrinsic importance resides in the seductive power which a good-for-nothing like Troy can exercise over such a woman as Bathsheba Everdene in *Far from the Madding Crowd.*

Troy is one of the most worthless of all the characters in these novels. A swashbuckler of vulgar aspect, this non-commissioned officer without scruples seems better fitted to make the conquest of some barmaid than a rich and intelligent manageress of a farm. Yet he proves stronger than the gentle Gabriel Oak and the ardent and respectful Boldwood.

The first meeting between Troy and Bathsheba is not devoid of romance. The scene takes place on the very edge of the farm. Lantern in hand the young woman has just been going her rounds. Suddenly under the dark canopy of a group of pines the nightwalker stumbles against a human form. The folds of her skirt are caught in the rowel of a spur. There is in this scene an element of symbolism which shews how a writer may realise the harmony existing between his plots as a novelist, weaving his intrigues, and his psychological views on sex. Before they know or have even seen one another, the two are already attached to each other. The tangling together of their garments is a forerunner of the intertwining of their souls. There is a note of brutality in the appearance of Sergeant Troy which the author compares to a trumpet-call heard amid the silence. The gallant soldier is not at home in the lists of love. He begins at once with direct flattery, addressing the most outspoken compliments to the pretty girl. The fellow's advances are not without an element of insolence and the lady of the farm is ill-pleased at her slightly ridiculous posture in this unexpected encounter. She gives vent to her annoyance but there is no pause in the flood of declarations of love. They soon take effect. What woman could forget the handsome soldier, who could find such words of leave-taking as " Ah, Beauty; good bye ! " At their next meeting the cavalier resumes the assault. The seduction is finally accomplished by means of a whirl-wind spectacle of sword-play which Troy offers to his lady, and which ends with the victory of the soldier who receives a kiss.[1]

A passion which deceives itself, blinds itself and finally loses itself in a maze of futile denials, only adding to the avowals already made, seizes upon this delicate creature. She becomes a mere plant torn up by the roots, but of that she will know nothing. She refuses to realise that there is no longer the slenderest thread to hold her to the earth.

[1] This scene is in the worst possible taste. One might compare it with a scene in " *A Laodicean*," in which Captain de Stancy, mimicking one of his ancestors pretends to run someone through with a rapier, in order to impress the young Paula. (Book III, Chap. II.)

Thus, without being directly under the domination of the instincts, while still dwelling among women who wish to struggle and to defend themselves, Bathsheba is none the less subjugated, like any farm-girl, and in the end it is the most masculine, if not the worthiest type that triumphs.

The mystery of the attractions, which place many human beings at the mercy and under the charm of certain individuals, reveals itself with all the force of a physiological shock, which declares itself in Hardy's work at the moment when the emotions of love first announce themselves. It is perhaps not impossible to find some explanation of this organic fatalism.

A disciple of Ribot, for example, might imagine some afflux of blood immediately neutralising several of the brain-centres and thereby giving rise to a state of complete monoideism. The mechanism of the phenomenon would continue to act with perfect simplicity, its whole force residing in its perfect effectiveness. The discharge would, in fact, hurl the beings under observation into the very heart of passion and intrigue, and thereby into the centre of their destiny and of their task in life. The decisive character of such a passion could never be called in question.

From the sentimental point of view love is an emotion which, in order to secure acceptance, persuades the individual that it brings happiness and pleasure, illusory benefits, when it be considered that they spell subordination to the species. Victims of this trickery, human beings always fall into the trap.

What then is the significance of the influences attributed to a kind of magic lodged by nature in human beings? These profane words allow of an interpretation which runs the risk of remaining purely verbal. Assuredly reason does not preside over the choice which is made in love. But that is not the only cause. Others may perhaps be distinguished in chiaroscuro. There is a kind of shadow-play, giving rise to zones into which the eye may not penetrate.

Reason evolves within its proper domain. Fast in the grip of their own reality, autonomous and common to them both, life and love are not subject to any rational order, springing from the categories of the intelligence. Life and love pursue their ardent course upon a plane different from that occupied by pure intellect and consciousness. But if that course be prolonged it cannot fail to join that other plane where omnipotent Will holds sway, the master of the world.

In all that concerns love, therefore, there are many actions for which intelligence cannot account.

CHAPTER VII

HARDY'S WOMEN

" Women go much further in love than the majority of men."

La Bruyère. Characters III.

" Varium et mutabile semper Femina."

Virgil. Aen. IV (569-70).

BUT of what manner are those women whose hearts we have already heard beating in the avowals preceding the formation of the couple ?

" Subtle in her simplicity,"[1] writes Hardy of one of his heroines. Elsewhere, he describes Paula[2] as a creature " half romantic, half worldly." We frequently meet with similar portrayals of the unconscious psychological tortuousness of some of his principal woman characters.[3] Reason plays a purely subaltern role in their conduct. If in Bathsheba Everdene (*Far From the Madding Crowd*), who feels so happy to learn from Sergeant Troy that she is

---

1 *The Romantic Adventures of a Milkmaid.*
2 *A Laodicean.*
3 Hardy's ideas on this point are enshrined in numerous passages. How does he express himself regarding Felicia Charmond? " If one word could have expressed Felicia Charmond, it would have been Inconsequence." (*The Woodlanders.* Chapter XXV).

beautiful, we find an element of femininity and an
intelligence too wary to allow unlimited sway to the
promptings of sex, there is still in all her acts a strain
of caprice which too often imposes silence upon the
commands of sound sense. And yet the author proclaims this woman to be " of the stuff of which great
men's mothers are made."

In the same way Hardy says of Cytherea Graye,
the heroine of *Desperate Remedies*, that her reason
played with her imagination as a young cat plays
with a dead bird. This inferiority explains the role
of love in the existence of these women. The desire
for admiration, which we behold in all of them indeed, but mostly highly developed in Fancy Day and
in Bathsheba Everdene, shews us that Nature herself acquaints them with the destined role of their
charm and with the power which it wields, at the
same time instructing them in its necessity. With
them a special kind of sensibility is always triumphant, whereas in the case of men intelligence tends
to emancipate. But this very sensibility accords to
love a wider role in a woman's life.

Here we may recall the famous utterance of
Madame de Stael : " Love is the whole history of a
woman's life : in the life of a man it is a mere
episode." Do we not find the same opinion expressed in Byron's *Don Juan* ?

> " Man's love is of man's life a thing apart,
>   'Tis woman's whole existence."

Woman's spontaneity is, in fact, the expression
and the condition of that will to live which determines
her destiny. In his earliest novel Hardy discovered

this corner-stone for the structure of his heroine's
psychology.

" A great statesman," he writes, " thinks several
times, and acts; a young lady acts, and thinks
several times."[1] Eustacia, Viviette, Lucetta, Felicia,
Arabella, all conjure forth from their desires the
sensual whirlpool of love. One is conscious of their
abdication before the master of their hearts and of
their submission to the fleshly instinct and to everything which must lead them to disaster. These are
the passion-driven among the women. But there are
also Sue, who is almost lacking in sex, Elizabeth-
Jane, Ethelberta, and the smiling group of girls who
belong to two lovers, such as Grace, Fancy, Elfride,
Paula, Ann, and many others whose coquetry and
feminine refinement make charming creatures of
them, and whose misfortune it is to be condemned
always to choose the inconstant or unworthy suitor
and to turn aside from a warm and more certain
affection. As Mr Hedgcock very justly observed in
the most exhaustive work yet devoted to Hardy,
for the frank and naive ardour of their passion the
women in his gallery are only comparable to Shakespeare's women, among them the charming Miranda,
Juliet with her pure and unblemished sensuousness,
and the fatal, sickly and luxurious Cleopatra. All
these women closely resemble their sisters in the
Wessex Novels, for their love is often a love that
knows no limits and is almost always born at first
sight. One might imagine oneself to be listening to
a Hardy heroine when Miranda cries out in the presence of Ferdinand : " I might call him a thing divine,
for nothing natural I ever saw so noble."[2]

[1] *Desperate Remedies.*   [2] *The Tempest.* Act I, Scene II.

By what is at least a curious and picturesque coincidence Hardy ascribes the sensuality of certain women to a partly foreign extraction. Shakespeare did the same. When he wished to introduce sensuality in his theatre, he sought his heroines in the warmer climates. Such are Juliet, Desdemona and Cleopatra. Mr Hedgcock has spoken of Shakespeare, but might one not also evoke the memory of Goethe's Marguerite, the greatest and the most grief-laden sister of all these women?

Hardy not only possessed the gift of divining souls. His heroines have a physical existence no less than a moral, and the links between their beauty and their character are forged by an artist eminently qualified to form creatures of flesh and blood, adjusted to the ends for which he strove.

Of all his women characters Tess is undoubtedly the most sympathetic and the most complete expression of woman as conceived by Hardy. A whole book grows out of this portrait, a book which deals exclusively with the history of this " pure woman." To the very end of the story the peasant woman continues to deserve this appellation. Betrayed by her ignorance and taken by surprise, Tess bows in subjection before the law of the male. She is for ever trembling in revolt and, moved by a sentiment perhaps not far from the disgust felt by Sue, she is conscious of an invincible repugnance towards the man who has corrupted her. It is this sentiment which guides the whole of her conduct and inspires her flight from Alec's acts of generosity. She recoils in horror from any pact of shame:

" I have said that I will not take anything from

you and I will not. I cannot: I should be your creature to go on doing that, and I won't."

A similar refusal suggested amazed reflections to one of Galsworthy's characters in *The Island Pharisees*. In this case it is the story of a village-girl seduced by a gamekeeper, from whom she refuses to accept any reparation.

George Moore's *Mere Accident* (1887) presents analogies both of character and situation, all the more interesting in that it preceded *Tess*. Just before her marriage, Kitty, a clergyman's daughter, is brutally violated by a tramp in a lonely spot. For a long time she does not understand, she does not " realise " what has happened. At length there dawns within her the idea of a supposed fault, driving her to suicide.

With Tess remorse and shame result much more from her situation as a girl who has been seduced than from within her conscience. She bears no responsibility for a sin which she has not committed, but of which she is rather the victim. Her fall costs her her place in society and the sense of the stigma imprinted upon her gives rise to the notion of an imaginary " mea culpa." This attitude Hardy disputes. He sees in the situation of which she is the victim one of the consequences of the Law of Nature and, so far from placing Tess outside Nature, he repeatedly tells her that she is in harmony, not at issue with her.

There is, however, in Tess a splendid animal luxuriance, a flowering of the flesh, a physical element which belies the purity of her spirit and intentions. Tess is the victim of that outward ripeness, which makes her the prey, with which an Alec desires to

sate his lust. To strengthen yet further this pre-
destination to downfall, Hardy adds to his heroine's
character a trait very deeply rooted in persons of
peasant stock, a certain carelessness, a readiness to
surrender under the pressure of the desires which
come roaming about her. It is one of the contrasts
of her nature that the nobility of her spirit, the
generosity of her heart, indeed all the qualities which
elevate her are compromised by her invincible weakness. The farm-girl thus stands opposed to Sue, who
incarnates thought and intellectual curiosity in a
spirit from which the sexual element is absent. Tess
is a creature abounding in life; Sue is immaterial.

Yet in Sue also we find a contrast of a similar
character, for it is in her nature to provoke that very
sexual desire which she regards with horror.

The unhappy destiny of Tess closely resembles
that of George Eliot's heroine in *Adam Bede*. Hetty
Sorrel, the girl who has been seduced, suffers the
supreme punishment for her act of infanticide.
Beautiful, amiable, childlike, coquettish and vain,
she is attracted to her own undoing towards everything that glitters. No real warmth of sentiment
dwells within the soul of this child-woman. To anything which is not ribbon or lace she reacts with a
kind of indifference. Behind a cloak of innocence
she conceals the same perversity which one observes in the milkmaid of Greuze. Thus Hetty
is a real sinner. She is " in fault," and she is
punished.

Hardy examines Tess's intentions. He shows us
the victim unjustly smitten. More of a preacher,
George Eliot curbs vice and rewards virtue. It is a
necessary consequence of these two attitudes that

two human beings, almost twins in respect of their destinies, are morally opposites.

Attracted by the sharpest crises Hardy excels in showing how far passion may be effective in bringing about transformation. And it is to this power that some of his characters owe it that their stature is increased and ennobled by passion. While still hovering amid her first sentimental uncertainties, Eustacia[1] hardly arouses any sympathy in the reader. It requires nothing less than a most unhappy adventure to adorn her brow with a halo of suffering.

What, then, is permanent in the character of the drama of a woman's heart? Because of passion we accompany her through every phase of a bitter conflict between instinct, which proclaims " love ", and intelligence, which answers with exhortations to " security " and " tranquillity."[2] Yet with these heroines of sensibility there can be no question but that instinct will triumph, and that, led astray by it, Hardy's women must for ever forego the taste of happiness. We must not, however, allow all these catastrophes to blind us to the real nature of the writer's dream. His own leanings are divulged by the subjects upon which his preference falls. His ideal is based upon the triple alliance of beauty, purity and intelligence, incarnated with an endless diversity of nuances alike in Tess and in Sue, in Fancy Day and in Grace Melbury and in all those young women, so numerous in his work, who are endowed with grace and with the powers of seduction. Destiny is not favourable to the flowering of

---

1 *The Return of the Native.*
2 This is an essential phase in that life and death struggle between flesh and spirit. (See the preface to *Jude the Obscure.*)

their delicate gifts; it does not conspire in their favour.

A place apart must be accorded to two of his heroines, who are in some sort exceptional in this world of women.

With Ethelberta interest directed by reason triumphs over the promptings of sentiment. Intelligent, courageous and obstinate, Ethelberta sacrifices the preference of her heart to the desire to assure her future and that of her family by means of a marriage which will secure her from all embarrassment. First and foremost a daughter and a sister, she presents the type of a finished realist in all that concerns marriage.

Then we have Elisabeth-Jane in *The Mayor of Casterbridge*. Her life is full of difficulties of every kind, but the young woman always knows how to face them. Her cool reason proves adequate to estimating simple and moderate satisfactions at their true value. She aspires to hold a middle course between the exaltation derived from over-great joys and the discouragement springing from painful disappointment. Avoiding these two extremes, she is inspired by a prudence which finally triumphs over numerous vicissitudes. Her conduct carries with it its own reward. An attitude of such reserve and perseverance always prevails against contrary winds. Must one not regret that Elisabeth-Jane's sisters, that all the women in Hardy's novels could not have meditated more fully upon such an example, one might say upon such a lesson? This truly Minerva-like figure is the sole creature in Hardy's works capable of confronting adversity with honour.

One's final impression in leaving this unique

gallery is that Hardy reveals himself as a true painter
of women, above all of girls. Perhaps he was too
much addicted to presenting among his female characters the type of the passionate animal, the creature
of pleasure, like those three maid-servants of Talbothays, who appear in the evening in their room all
burning with desire for Angel Clare. " The differences which distinguished them as individuals were
abstracted by this passion, and each was but portion
of one organism called sex."

This passage may be compared with certain other
lines in Hardy, occurring in *Desperate Remedies*. As
he watches the two rivals, Cytherea Graye and Miss
Hinton, at grips with each other, the author ex-
claims: " The situation abstracted the differences
which distinguished them as individuals, and left
only the properties common to them as atoms of a
sex." Already in a previous passage in the same
book he had written in that favourite style of his:
" Concentrated essence of women pervaded the
room."

It results from such traits as these that woman
tends to identify herself too completely with the
mere creature of love, which in fact she is not always.[1]
And in this respect Hardy's great heroines resemble
one another perhaps too closely. This is the source
alike of their weakness and of their grandeur. A
mighty flame burns within them and its flickerings
express the quiverings of their spirits and the palpi-

[1] Hardy was no doubt anxious to correct the element of excess
in his attitude. He makes Sue say to Jude, who is astonished at
her aversion for the physiological side of love. " I am not so exceptional a woman as you think. Fewer women like marriage than
you suppose, only they enter into it for the dignity it is assumed
to confer."

tations of their hearts, making of them the most wonderful among the daughters of the Eternal Eve.

These creatures owe their captivating seductiveness to the decrees of the caprice which governs their actions. But, in reality, these decrees are predetermined. They express the will to live. They are issued subject to a law of necessity which, with this novelist, links the action with the intimate structure of the character.

If Hardy chooses this trait as the most conclusive in woman's character, he thereby demonstrates more amply that the action takes its rise in the very source of the emotion itself, to terminate in a tragic result wherein everything is destroyed. In the final analysis it is from this little seed of madness that the first impulse starts, sovereign and instinctive, hurling these women upon the slope down which they slide at the bidding of natural laws, without the slightest regard for the conscious desires which still survive in them.

From this we see how everything in Hardy's works presents itself as an ordered whole and how, by his gifts as a painter of the character of woman with all its sudden changes of humour, the writer has shown that he could bend all the springs of the human spirit in the direction of his chosen aims. Hardy is, therefore, above all a painter of women. Nothing indeed is as rare as a writer capable of depicting with equal success the characters of both sexes. Hardy does not handle masculine psychology with the same penetration. His male characters are either sensual or effeminate, or else victims of a kind of internal attrition. He doubtless discovered in woman a complexity which remained more prominently before his

eyes, a submission to instinct which involved her in
more intimate relations with the whole ordering of
things. His imagination found a field more open for
a series of adventures in a region essentially belonging to his art. Thanks to the diversity permitted it,
passion assumes more individual forms and on each
occasion develops like an original organism upon the
groundwork of a mighty unity.

How did Hardy acquire this subtle and concrete
knowledge of the feminine heart which makes him
one of the masters of our time? Was not this gift
of divination which he possessed born of his first
experiences when he amused himself by acting as
friend and secretary to the girls of his village, as
Ernest Brennecke tells us in his work, in the chapter
devoted to the writer's childhood.[1]

The adolescent limited himself to holding the pen
and transcribing the natural expression of love as he
heard it upon lips trembling with passion. His rôle
in no way resembled that of Samuel Richardson, who
was himself responsible for the composition of the
letters. One wonders what wage Hardy received for
his good offices. No doubt he found it agreeable to
be close to a pretty girl, and perhaps, like Eustacia
Vye's young admirer, he sometimes for a few minutes
held the hand of a fair neighbour as a reward for one
of those precious services. All his sympathy springs
from the affection which he feels for these radiant
daughters of Nature. It is well known that Mr
Hardy had no liking for such explanations and dis-
puted them. In his eyes the creator can and should
find his material outside the substance of his own life.
Whenever a critic claimed to establish a connection

[1] *The Life of Thomas Hardy* (See Bibliography).

between an episode or character in his work and some experience in the author's own life, the solitary of Max Gate gave vent to his disapproval.

Whatever use Hardy may have made of other personal experiences is a secret which he guarded jealously during his lifetime. But unintentionally, and while still upholding Hardy's denials, Mrs Florence Hardy's book supplies us with many useful hints regarding the origin of facts observed or experienced and later transferred to the poems or novels.

Yet however jealous the novelist may have been in regard to his methods of work and to the sources of his inspiration, one none the less finds in Elfride, in *A Pair of Blue Eyes*, his first wife, Emma Lavinia Gifford, who was proud of being the niece of Archdeacon Gifford and made her husband feel it.

In support of this thesis, it is permissible to recognise in the architect's assistant, Stephen Smith, Thomas Hardy himself, the pupil of Sir Arthur Blomfield, so eager for learning and instruction.

One must not strive at all costs to hear the persistent echo of personal sufferings in the often disillusioned tone in which the poet and novelist speaks. However pessimistic he was, Hardy must none the less have been happy, and we should not forget this confession, marked by a noble pride and a great purity of heart, contained in verses which one feels must refer to the poet himself :

" Whatever his message—glad or grim—
Two bright-souled women clave to him."[1]

The allusion to the two companions of his life is transparent and significant.

[1] A Poet.—*Satires of Circumstance.*

Besides, in spite of her weaknesses and her contradictions, woman is the great vanquished in love, and Hardy throughout all his work bends with a sort of solicitude over her lot as an eternal victim.

Could one write a more beautiful epitaph upon woman's heart?

" A woman's heart has room for one alone,
A man's for two or three.
Centred is woman's love and knows no breadth."[1]

[1] *The Famous Tragedy of the Queen of Cornwall.*

CHAPTER VIII

FROM THE CONFLICT OF THE SEXES TO THE FORMATION OF THE PAIR

MARRIAGE AND SEXUAL LIFE

" From the moment at which it is concluded and sealed marriage is a thing which has yet to be created, not a state already in being."

ALAIN.

Eighty-one chapters upon the Human Spirit and the Passions. *On Marriage.*

AFTER examining the fragile relations between man and woman with such a merciless regard for truth, Hardy could not remain indifferent to the social aspects and consequences of the conflict of the sexes.

The Victorian era had chanted the dithyramb of marriage. It celebrated the indissoluble union wherein woman became at once the private property of her husband,[1] and, as with Coventry Patmore, *The Angel in the House.* This panegyric consecrated the semi-effacement of the woman within the honourable framework of the family and of duty. As George Meredith showed in *The Egoist,* countless Sir Willoughbys demanded of the girl the innocence of a

[1] See John Stuart Mill—*The Subjection of Women.* Dewes— " The injustice of the English Law as it bears on the Relationship of Husband and Wife."

118

newly-hatched bird! At the end of the preceding
century, however, William Godwin and his wife,
Mary Wollstonecraft, had in the name of Reason
sought to reform the accepted principles of morality
and, in particular, marriage. But their innovating
doctrines had not left the slightest furrow in the
atmosphere. *A Vindication of the Rights of Woman*,
which Mary Wollstonecraft published in 1792, had
long previously been forgotten.

A revision of current ideas was now imperative. It
could not be postponed at a moment when literature
was approaching all subjects with the deliberate aim
of contesting out-worn dogmas. Yet it was only in
1882 that the English woman acquired civil personality in the eyes of the law.[1]

The century took no account officially of the rights
of the wife. A great material prosperity seemed to
veil all the harshness of legislation. And yet Tennyson's chimerical vision, as it appeared in *The Princess*
in 1849, summoned the woman to an affectionate
collaboration, and the Utopia prepared the way for
the reality, for woman's admission to the liberal pro-
fessions, and even for the extension of her social rôle.
From Charles Reade to Mrs Humphrey Ward the
novel continued faithful to this gospel. In Hardy's
case the realist may perhaps have been said to neglect
the purely feminist aspect of certain themes in order
to explore human relation with fearless eyes, to investigate the element of trickery in them, and merci-
lessly to lay bare the reverse of the medal of respected
institutions.

Marriage, proclaims Hardy uncompromisingly, is a
passing instinct, which it is sought to render per-

[1] The Married Woman's Property Act.

manent by means of an oath.[1] In *The Woodlanders*
one of his characters, Dr Edred Fitzpiers, declares
not without cynicism, " Marriage is a civil contract,
and the simpler and shorter, the better."

We are now in an atmosphere very far removed
from the famous and oft-quoted text of Modestinus :
" Nuptiae sunt conjunctio maris et feminae et con-
sortium omnis vitae, divini et humani juris com-
municatio."[2]

Does this, however, mean that in the *Wessex
Novels* one meets with the systematic criticism of an
institution ? Assuredly not. The writer has nothing
of the controversialist in him. He always refused to
assume a combative attitude. In one of his prefaces[3]
he gladly shielded himself behind the authority of
Gibbon to assert that, like the historian, the novelist
must not intrude his own judgment upon the facts
which he presents. However sincere Hardy may
have been in claiming this objectivity, it is none the
less true that his eye acquired a species of discipline.
At certain hours it could only see certain things, from
which a whole train of thought proceeded. The
writer never advances to the attack, but the discoveries which he presents are overwhelming. They
constitute at once charge and proof. While from the
social point of view marriage is no doubt unassail-
able, when it is opposed to the moral expansion of
the individual, it becomes one of the most grievous
of yokes ; and this Hardy has recorded with merciless
force and irony.

1 *Jude the Obscure.*
2 " Marriage is a joining together of husband and wife, a part-
nership which endures throughout the whole of life, a communica-
tion of divine and human law."
3 *The Woodlanders.*

Moreover, this impassivity did not prevent him from formulating, in the short preface to *The Woodlanders*, the phrase which expresses the problem in its true equation : ". . . the question of matrimonial divergence, the immortal puzzle, given the man and woman how to find a basis for their sexual relation," and the problem is too closely contained in the terms which he employs for it to be eluded in what follows. The *Wessex Novels* in fact put before us the author's vision of the pair rather than any exposition of a system. "Let me repeat," he declares in the preface to the fifth edition of *Tess*, "that a novel is an impression, not an argument." Hardy is not a doctrinaire of the stamp of Brieux.

He does not set out to sap the foundations of the institution itself. He is concerned rather with the merciless exposure of the heart-breaking results of ill-assorted unions, which a malignant destiny has found it pleasant to arrange. "The mire of marriage," such are the words with which Eustacia, aghast at the threats of an insane husband, dares one day to accuse marriage itself of being the cause of all their sufferings.[1]   Tortured at heart Eustacia never loved the man whom she married. She was in love with love and marriage was to be for her deliverance, intoxication and joy. The loss of her illusion spelled death to her.

It is essential for our purpose to become acquainted with the nature of the criticism which the writer was able to advance, as one who had examined and understood the problem.

Marriage is a social rite implying the effacement of the individual. Jude twice sacrifices himself to

[1] *The Return of the Native.*

it, immolating his dreams and his plans for raising
himself. One thing in all this seems prodigiously
hateful and ridiculous in the author's eyes, it is that
solemn oath that all feelings, beliefs and desires shall
be held fast within the harmony demanded by the
law of two beings naturally inconstant. Sue revolts
at the very idea of again pronouncing such vows.
" To love some man or woman all one's life is tanta-
mount to saying that a candle can go on burning for
ever," says Pozdnycher in the *Kreutzer Sonata*.[1]

In what a state of perturbation Hardy's characters
make this essay of happiness. One might almost say
that they were seeking a kind of suicide. For women
like Eustacia and Viviette it is a way of playing one
of the cards of life crazily and impulsively. All is
risked to gain all, but probably to lose all.

What still remains in the face of the bankruptcy
of marriage ?

In *Jude the Obscure* we are confronted with the
problem of free love. Each in turn, Sue and Jude,
the two criticizing spirits, come with their statements
of injury. Each has a pseudo-scientific mentality and
their semi-intellectualism conducts them to anarchy.

For the heroine of the book marriage seems an
insupportable regime and the two insurgents decide
to seek their happiness without any desire to legalise
it. Both are making their second attempt to live in
common with another and yet this new effort does
not even yield an apology for a free union. It is not
enough to escape from the social rite and the con-
straint which it implies if one would taste of happiness on the basis of an act of selection, freed from
all element of formalism. Sue and Jude, on the other

1 See Chapter II.

hand, show themselves just as unfit for free union as for marriage, which both have abandoned. The attempt made with the enthusiasm of fanaticism only ends in a most dramatic catastrophe. The passengers have ventured themselves upon too frail a bark. The second crossing offers too many dangers and the result is shipwreck. After all these catastrophes one is more in the mood to hear the counsel for prosecution than the arguments for the defence.

The problem of free union is not the only one which we encounter in this book where so many ideas jostle one another. The question of the sexual relations between married persons plays an equally prominent role. In Jude we see the semi-rustic in whom a single look from Arabella has aroused the instincts of the male. Once weaned from the very earthly sustenance which he had derived from that heady girl, he again falls under the dominion of his dreams of conquest in the sphere of learning. He believes that he may soon crown them with the image of a woman and rejoins his highly educated cousin Sue. Both are sprung from a stock which is notorious for its matrimonial failures. They are attempting the impossible. Sue is so entirely devoid of sex that she proposes to Jude a fraternal communion of minds, unattended by any fleshly tie. In the strangeness of this situation there lies a paradoxical idea touching one of the gravest problems of married life. Sue asserts that what is most horrible in marriage is the obligation resting upon the woman to respond at all moments to the man's desires. This evasion on the part of the woman, who in response to a deeply-seated sensibility refuses to admit certain contacts, powerfully attracted the writer. He incarnated this morbid case in a heroine who although of ethereal nature was yet true to life.

Virgin Soil, by George Egerton (Mrs Golding Bright)), shows us another woman whose attitude offers certain analogies with the repugnance evinced by Sue. Florence charges marriage with being a legal prostitution which hands over the wife to the demands of the husband, investing him with permanent rights to obtain from his companion what he must beg or buy from his mistress. This theme, indeed, does to some extent recall the objections put forward by Sue. *Virgin Soil* is the work of a disciple of Maupassant and of the French naturalists.

When studying the criticism of marriage as it appears in Hardy's novels and when comparing it with other criticisms, we do not pretend that it is either new or original. Already, in 1851, in her short preface to *Mauprat*, George Sand reproached marriage with its excessive resemblance to a " contract of material interests." " The ideal of love," she continues, " is certainly eternal fidelity. Moral and religious laws have sought to consecrate that ideal; material facts beset its path and civil laws are often so framed as to render it impossible or illusory. . . ."

All these words sound in strange contradiction with those with which at the beginning of *Middlemarch* George Eliot unctuously salutes marriage as " the beginning of the home epic." Nothing must loosen the marriage tie. There must not even be any question of it.

Far from the Madding Crowd, if published anonymously, might have been attributed to the author of *Adam Bede*. Yet Hardy is entirely lacking in sentimentalism. Disillusioned as he is, he remains a

spirit of profound sanity. Without ever assuming
the tone or the bearing of a " Quaker," he expresses
himself with the detachment and authority of an
observer who looks even beyond human destiny.

The prose-writer was often aware of and indicated
the salutary   elements which must be brought together to form a healthy union. In the concise language familiar to him, at the very moment of writing
these aphorisms he found a formula in which he resumed those conditions. In order that the pair may
be able to resist the assaults of life it is essential that
it should realise a " sympathetic inter-dependence,
wherein mutual weaknesses are made the grounds of
a defensive alliance."[1] Unhappily all idea of such
an agreement is absent from the human beings whom
he pits against one another.

Only events and the chastisement which they have
in store become—but all too late—a terrible school
in which the truth is revealed.

Fitzpiers passes through a valley of tears in redemption of his faults. An unfaithful husband,
whose adventures with Suke and Felicia have inflicted grievous hurt upon Grace's affection, he can
only regain her gradually by treading the road of
contrition. One can imagine the two later, a
pair that is often melancholy; for Grace will assuredly never forget the sacrifice by which Winterborne has been immolated, her heroic and platonic
cavalier.

Two others reach, tardily enough, a quiet haven.
But that again was after many trials and vicissitudes.
In *Far From the Madding Crowd* Bathsheba who has
disdained the love of Gabriel and uselessly provoked

1 *The Woodlanders.*

that of the farmer Boldwood lets herself be seduced
by a libertine non-commissioned officer who has the
manners of a Don Juan . . . . Later the only happiness she knows is that which springs from a kind of
affectionate compromise with the shepherd Gabriel.
After such experiences the pair can no longer be a
sentimental improvisation, happy and without a
morrow. It will be a far more serious consummation,
a union of all the conditions indispensable to the
stability of happiness. When fully ripe, the harvest
of wisdom is gathered in after such proofs as the death
of Fanny Robin, the murder of Troy and the imprisonment of Boldwood. So many misfortunes do
not occur without design. They show us that we
are not in the best of all possible worlds. But by
the time that this sorry climax has been reached
Bathsheba and Gabriel have become tried friends.
The shams and the coquetries which mark the conflict of the sexes are no longer becoming in such a
union as theirs. A profound sentiment brings them
together. After the shocks of tragedy the cooing
notes of a love duet can no longer be expected.
And the writer concludes : " This good fellowship—
camaraderie—usually occurring through similarity
of pursuits, is unfortunately seldom superadded to
love between the sexes, because men and women
associate not in their labours, but in their pleasure
merely."[1]

Here are maxims and precepts packed with good
sense and experience, against the moment when their
enunciation shall seem appropriate.

But in many cases the conclusions desultorily appended to some of the novels seem like a kind of

[1] *Far from the Madding Crowd.* Chap. XVI.

transient concession to the tradition which demands
an ending in marriage to reassure the optimists. The
marriage which in the last pages unites the patient
Diggory Venn and the amiable Thomasin or that of
Gabriel and Bathsheba offer such epilogues in complete contrast with the general tone of the book.
Serial publication in a magazine rendered it essential
that the author should not run too far counter to the
reader's habits. For similar reasons Molière employed such devices. By what is clearly a mere
artifice he avoids pushing home the lesson which he
derives from his characters and escapes amid the
postures of a pirouette.

In Hardy, therefore, we sometimes encounter con-
ventional " dénouements ". It is only in some of the
novels that these excessively accommodating settle-
ments occur. No one can be misled in regard to their
significance, for they in no way alter the writer's
views upon marriage. On this topic he did not refrain
from giving utterance to sayings which bear the mark
of a well-tempered intelligence steeped in a harsh,
even pitiless wisdom.

Conjugal happiness can only be attained through
an understanding based on mutual concessions. To
adopt the expression employed by Hardy in *An
Imaginative Woman,* there is no possibility of harmony between two people, unless they can find a
" common denominator " applicable to all their
tastes and desires.[1]

The broadest and most positive conclusion arrived
at after much criticism is that marriage should not

---

1 " It was to their tastes and fancies, those smallest, greatest
particulars, that no common denominator could be applied." *An
Imaginative Woman.*

be made an indissoluble tie, which, as the novelist wrote in a post-script to the preface to *Jude*, imposes a useless cruelty on both parties.[1] This seems to lie at the roots of the writer's thought.

In the same way as a poet he wrote in *The Famous Tragedy of the Queen of Cornwall at Tintagel in Lyonnesse*.

> " Why did Heaven warrant in its whim
> A twain mismated should bedim,
> The courts of their encompassment
> With bleeding loves and discontent."

In connection with this topic the novelist avails himself of an opportunity occurring in *An Imaginative Woman* to attack marriages of expediency and the claim to get " life leased at all cost," an offence which many mothers have committed against their children. Hardy, on the other hand, considers that for a woman, celibacy is preferable to an ill-adjusted marriage and that it is a more effective safeguard of her interests, dignity and freedom.[2] Marriage does not constitute the ultimate end of life. It is merely a stage upon the road of existence. To seek to make it the supreme aim is to condemn human beings to an allegedly civilized but really barbaric form of slavery. These ideas appear in Hardy's books and if they do not constitute their main interest, they are none the less the expression of a philosophy, this time positive, which teaches by what road one may escape so many disasters.[3]

---

1 " A marriage should be dissoluble, as soon as it becomes a cruelty to either of the parties—being then essentially and morally no marriage."

2 Hardy refuses to admit " that a bad marriage with its aversions is better than free womanhood."—*Life's Little Ironies*.

3 See Annexes pp. 208-9.

When marriage has made the pair a social reality, the romance is over and done with, the author observes humorously. Dick Dewy looks with amazement upon his parents who have become so prosaic. Why have they not always remained lovers?

Knowing little of life, too many of his characters dream, on the contrary, of an impossible happiness and fate does not forgive those who seek to force from her her secret by treading paths which she has not marked out. The men who really know how to love like Giles Winterborne, Diggory Venn, and Gabriel Oak are rare. And what does fate do for them? Gabriel Oak loves Bathsheba, who loves Troy. Diggory Venn loves Thomasin, who loves Wildeve. Giles Winterborne loves Grace, who loves Fitzpiers, and to add to it all, these three men, after the manner of Dick Dewy, are guilty of the fault of loving women above their respective stations, women who are their superiors in education and knowledge. But if such men who really love are not loved in return, it is because they and others with them, such as Edward Springrove, Clym Yeobright, Stephen Smith, are not men of action but remain dreamers lacking in will and audacity. But Hardy's women, sometimes sensual, often haughty, always coquettes, prefer conquering spirits to poetical novices and humble adorers. Conscious of this inferiority his heroines seem to agree with Jouffroy's phrase in *Le Cahier Vert*, "Constancy is a kind of impotence."

We see them standing amid the interplay of principles of selection already envisaged in a kind of penumbra. In a passage in *La Gaya Scienzia* Nietzsche wrote that woman wishes to be taken and accepted as a form of property, that she desires a man who seizes without abandoning himself, one who can enrich his ego by means of an increment of force and pleasure. Such an idea throws light upon the ascendancy of certain men and upon the character of the sway which they hold over certain mentalities.

This influence, at times quite magnetic, is so real that the timidity of a Stephen Smith or a Giles Winterborne has less effect upon Elfride and Grace than the harsh and instructed mastery of a Knight or a Fitzpiers. In both cases the issue is substantially the same; it is only the episodes that are different. A Grace Melbury does not hesitate between the simple faith of a Winterborne and the seductive powers of a Fitzpiers. Like the painter Jocelyn Pierston in *The Well-Beloved* Stephen Smith in *A Pair of Blue Eyes* does not know how to wish and to obtain. Elfride finds her master in Knight.

Hardy, then, could not believe in the equality of the sexes. At no time had he an unlimited faith in the emancipation of women. In his eyes the young girl, even when liberated, was destined to become a matron. No progress, therefore, is possible.[1] The picture which he draws of the conditions amid which the woman herself accords favour or submits to the choice suggested by Nature shows to what an extent she is a serf.

It was, moreover, the theme of the hour. Without being a misogynist of the brand of Schopenhauer, Hardy could not escape from the literary and philosophical setting of his time. It is interesting to compare his attitude with a passage of Wilkie Collins in *Man and Wife*, a novel which appeared in 1870:

1 *The Well-Beloved.*

"However persistently the epicene theorist of modern times may deny it, it is nevertheless a truth plainly visible in the whole past history of the sexes that the natural condition of a woman is to find her master in a man. The possession of a master is the only possible completion of their lives." This inferiority entails upon the woman many cruel deceptions. The weight of this necessity bears down all possibility of her becoming the clear-sighted creature who is capable of choosing a companion worthy of her.

Such is the ransom imposed by Nature. What will be that demanded by society with its constraints and prejudices? Society engenders new sources of conflict. Nature has swept away before the flood of passion many fragile and artificial barriers. But society awaits the hour of her revenge, for she does not pardon those who have transgressed her decrees, even if they have done so involuntarily. Deep in the shadows the prejudices still continue their existence, lowering like assassins on the watch. Beneath the hail of blows which they deal the human pair is again menaced with the risk of perishing. After knowing the excesses of the Law of Nature, which demands the unchaining of passions, the pair is subjected to rigours of the social law which exacts respect for the conventions.

In many cases the final triumph of respect for society completes the ruin of happiness already compromised. The woman is often at once the initiator and the victim. Thus when Sue abandons Jude at the death of their children, she thinks of nothing but rejoining her first husband. Remorse and an overwhelming need for fidelity bring her back to the first duty which, according to her conscience, she ought

never to have betrayed. Something forces her away
from Jude like that longing for sincerity, basically
a rather paltry thing, which takes Tess away from
Angel Clare and bids her avow the defilement which
she has undergone at the hands of Alec. Cytherea,
too, on the very eve of marrying Manston still
struggles against everything that attaches her to
Springrove. Deep within her there lives on a respect
for the word which she has given. Elsewhere we
see other contests, in the man's heart, too, and in
his case the triumph of social prejudice is complete.
Angel, the parson's son, abandons Tess when he learns
to his despair that she is not the pure creature of
his dreams. Thrust back for a time, where it is a
question of the poor girl's humble circumstances,
prejudice reappears triumphant at the avowal of the
stigma. In *A Pair of Blue Eyes*, Henry Knight
severs himself from Elfrida whom he loves, when his
romantic desire for an absolute purity of heart in
woman is deceived. He rejects Elfride's ardent love,
when he learns that she has allowed Smith to make
advances. Thus Angel Clare and Henry Knight,
those two " enlightened " thinkers, are deplorably
alike one another. Angel loves in Tess " the virginal
daughter of Nature." He loves a kind of ideal ab-
straction, not a woman. His concrete sensibility is
chilled by the deductions of his reasoning power.
Under the influence of that he no longer perceives
the treasures of tenderness which he is flinging away.
He dominates his egoism only when it is too late.
Angel it pitiless. Not for a moment can he understand what he is losing. Notwithstanding that she
has strayed, the spirit of Tess remains immaculate,
but how should he be aware of it caught up in the

wimple of his prejudices? Yet, he has some experience of life, the experience derived from his own love adventure, which he has confessed. Knight, that other unjust man, has at least this in his favour that he does not incur the same reproach. But Angel is lacking in generosity and large-mindedness. No feeling of pardon can penetrate to his consciousness. On the contrary, is it not in order to exact vengeance for the deception caused him by Tess that he proposes to elope with Izz Huett? What an ironical situation—to behold the man thus trampling under foot the very rules to which he claims to subject the woman!

Thus with the male characters the egoism of love and the cruelty of jealousy are often the two forces which complement one another to crown misfortune. For we find a great company of undisciplined spirits given up to an utter and unmitigated egoism, and enslaved to the forces of desire. Such are Manston, Wildeve, Troy, Fitzpiers and finally Alec d'Urbervilles, who ends amid the degradation of hypocrisy.

The writer has insisted with special stress upon the harmful effects of egoism. A sacred egoism, it may be objected, if one considers only the individual. A fatal egoism in the eyes of anyone who is concerned to see the pair fulfil its mission. "Selfishness," he writes in *The Return of the Native*, "is frequently the chief constituent of the passion, and sometimes its only one."

Its destructive force is a particularly dangerous weapon in the hands of intellectuals. With them the cult of the ego has perhaps developed a propensity to sacrifice everything to the personality. But Hardy has also laid his finger with a sure touch upon the

other causes. In *Two on a Tower* he expresses himself in the following terms upon this point : " He was
a scientist and took words literally. There is something in the inexorably simple logic of such men
which partakes of the cruelty of the laws that are
their study." The great fault of such men is that
they understand nothing of women whose mentality
is beyond the limits of logic.

In his book, *Characters and Environment in the
Novels of Thomas Hardy* (1925), Mr H. C. Grimsditch
quotes a sentence of Burke from his *Letter to a noble
Lord*; " Nothing can be conceived more hard than
the heart of a thoroughbred metaphysician." That
is why the love of a Saint-Cleeve, absorbed in the
contemplation of the heavens, can never match that
of the woman who loves him, Viviette, who knows no
other stars but the eyes of the young astronomer.

It is in virtue of such views upon the human heart,
often according with the surest observations of
thinkers and moralists, that Hardy's work acquires
its range and importance as a testimony on life.

We have already said that the men who are really
capable of love are very few. Gabriel Oak, Diggory
Venn and Giles Winterborne are almost alone in
possessing this genius which knows how to cherish
and to wait, and for a long time this affectionate
constancy clashes with the woman's sentimental
blindness. Their philosophy of patience constitutes
an all too rare exception.

A rigorous determinism presides over the formation and development of all these characters. They
cannot escape the powerful causality which raises its
head everywhere in Hardy's text. Often they have
their foundations in atavistic influences which, in

Jude and Sue for example, are the conditions of unfitness for a reasonable life and explain their chronic state of indecision. Other elements, too, play their part on this stage.

In Clym Yeobright dwells a son of Egdon Heath, fashioned by that vast and savage expanse even as the plants which grow there.[1] This man, who like Jude becomes an autodidact, unconsciously tainted with Rousseauism, loves the Heath which is his cradle as much as Eustacia, a transplanted creature who has never become acclimatized, detests and abhors it.

Elsewhere it is the implacable will of destiny, calling circumstances into play which triumph over the heart. The heart is at the mercy of combinations of events which render all insurgent efforts of the individual ineffective. The rôle of the passions is in no way diminished. For with Alec, Wildeve and Troy sensuality is dominant; it stifles the intelligence. When man is hot upon the chase of an object that he would possess, he is entirely consumed by his need. It puts an end to conscious life. In the cases of many of the male characters, love makes a kind of irruption, like an intruder. At the first onset the intelligence becomes a natural enemy. And yet according to the law of Nature, passion holds the field. Amid his inner conflict, face to face with the flesh, the man no longer contemplates the end towards which he advances as an individual. He becomes one with the male species which opposes him to the female, whose first instinct is a will to live derived from her

1 " He was permeated with its scenes, with its substances, and with its odours. He might be said to be its product." *The Return of the Native.*

hereditary functions. With the man the internal conflict arises from the fact that, in virtue of his more pronounced individuality, he is at once a member of a species and a species all by himself. Thus in Hardy one finds the conflict between will and intelligence which Schopenhauer has described. This opposition results from the presence of these two tendencies, which perhaps express two aspects of one and the same thing. A similar conflict arises from the dualism of knowing and acting. Intelligence also no doubt took its rise in the will to live. It probably represents a more perfect outcome of it and realises the highest and most fully developed aspiration of the will to fashion the world according to a desired image.

Hardy has shown us how the power of masculine attraction operates upon the woman. He has explained the character of feminine allurement for the man. He even composed a long symbolical tale on the pursuit of the eternal woman. In *The Well-Beloved* he personifies the pursuit of the immortal Eve in an incorrigible, imaginative, unsatisfied hero. Pierston places the diadem of his dreams of love upon the brow of every woman. Experiencing thrice over the same ideal emotion accompanied by the same headlong precipitation, he reincarnates the woman whom he has loved first in the daughter, then in the granddaughter of the original woman, who has disappeared. It is one of those imaginative stories in which fantasy reigns supreme, perhaps the better to express the author's thought.

When such precautions are observed in the shaping of the chief characters and in guiding their amorous development, there can no longer be any question of

the presence of free will in them.[1] The human pair
remains subject to the great laws which govern
animal life. Marriage is a very fragile bridge thrown
over too many abysses. The problem of its dura-
tion and its effectiveness is no longer put before us.
Frequently this legal and religious union is nothing
but a mere chain to break. We watch the escape
of the prisoners. It is a mere episode in the conflict
of the sexes. In the arena of life two beings encounter one another like gladiators, and the author
would gladly say to the reader: "Morituri te
salutant."

A sentence of Darwin, which must be quoted,
throws light upon more than one aspect of this serious
discussion. It is one of those at the end of his work
on the descent of man and sexual selection : "Man
scans with scrupulous care the character and pedigree
of his horses, cattle and dogs when he matches them ;
but when he comes to his marriage he rarely or never
takes such care." For his marriage it would seem
that he listens to the obscure instincts of the jungle,
or if he does escape their promptings, it is often only
to stop before considerations of secondary importance referring to fortune or social position. These
latter again turn us aside from the only rational
path. Once we leave it, our poor humanity seeks in
vain for a lasting and moderate solution of the problem raised by the union of the sexes, if it be desired
that the couple should be fit to found a family.

A stupid chance decrees that two ill-assorted
creatures should be united by ties of the flesh.

---

1 See the preface to "*Jude the Obscure*." "This man does
not act in a certain way by accident. His personality has been
moulded, for better or for worse, by agencies far more potent than
the individual will."

Nature takes part in the conspiracy, but it is only to satisfy the instincts, not to bring content to the soul. "The man to love rarely coincides with the hour of loving "[1], wrote Hardy with the powerful conciseness which grips his style at those moments when his hero's future is at stake. This sober commentary of the psychologist and moralist sums up the tremendous role played by chance in the formation oi the pair. Nature provides the man or the woman with a partner who is not fitted to be a companion with whom the other can live in harmony. The aphorism already quoted is one of these which bear the stamp of Hardy's genius as an analyst and a man of vision for all that touches upon the life of the flesh. With its implacable truth the phrase pours ridicule upon the invincible "tentatively" of the relations which may occur between a man and a woman in this framework of reality and imagination.

For it is into this "tentatively" that individuals stumble. Nature is content with chances and deals out irony or malice with a liberal hand. She delivers up Jude to Arabella, she abandons the spirit to the flesh. She surrenders Tess to Alec, she flings purity at the feet of lust.

The fall of Tess, astray and slumbering in the wood, entirely at the mercy of Alec's designs, becomes the dramatic moment of a conspiracy. Sleep, weariness, darkness and solitude, all offer their services to the felon.

The moment becomes invested with a kind of muffled solemnity. Thanks to fatal surroundings an act is about to be accomplished, the consequences of which can never be obliterated.

[1] *Tess of the d'Urbervilles.*

Where does the girl's guardian angel keep his watch? Where wanders that Providence in which she has put her faith? Idle questions.

Flesh, tempting and soft as velvet, is offered and innocence affords no shield as once to Una in Spensser's poem. It is the gazelle in the claws of the beast of prey, the virgin in the monstrous embrace of lust.

In this poignant scene, which makes sombre chance the artisan whose duty is to provide every living being with a companion, we see the spectacle of innocence abandoned by aid from on high and the evocation, the eternal recurrence of the things of this world, of just such other rapes perpetrated by some turbulent, debauched ancestor of Tess, returning to his manor after an encounter in coat of mail.

Desertion of the Gods? Ransom of the past? Cruel destinies of the flesh? Does the interpretation lie here?

Everything works to hand over an immaculate body to the pollutions of the male animal. Lending her criminal aid Nature unites two utterly unlike beings in a moment of madness. She mocks at them and their hopes. The purest diamond is buried in the peat. And yet after so many thousands of years no plausible explanation seems to offer itself save that of the malice inherent in things and in the whole universe.

Where find more deeply moving words than in the pathetic " finale " to the first movement of the sonata of desire and pity that bears the name of *Tess of the d'Urbervilles*?

CHAPTER IX

THE HUMAN PAIR AMID THE STORM OF CIRCUMSTANCE

" Beauty will never be a natural product; it can only appear as a result of artificial constraints."

ANDRE GIDE.

AN architect by profession Hardy always retained a taste for construction in his novels. In his work intrigue is not the result of any extempore improvisation. On the contrary one sees everywhere the plan of the architect, the conscious will of the builder revealed with all the traits of the perfect science of expression. The presence of the same influence is felt in the works of Sir John Vanbrugh, the architect of Blenheim and of the Haymarket, whose comedies show the builder's talent in the superiority of their framework. As a writer, moreover, whose descriptions are so much enriched by authentic traits of observation, both visual and auditory, and are traced upon a scantily disguised topographical ground work, Hardy is at no time a servile realist. Alike whether it is his task to imagine or to combine episodes, or to set foot upon the domain of the psychologist, he is never content with a mere registration of facts or reproduction of types. In every scene all the elements are distorted. His manner of knitting events together and of thus fixing their general direction makes him a kinsman of the historian Gibbon. The author of *The Decline and Fall of the Roman Empire* knew how to use fact and document, introducing between them and the past which he wished to resuscitate his own decisive personality. As M. Cazamian well expresses it, Gibbon felt himself "invested with plenary powers for the due ranging of facts."[1] Like Hardy, the historian harboured a strange conjunction of the scientific spirit and a vision at the same time synthetic and partial. It was in virtue of this that both were able to shape those mighty structures which reveal at once the extent of their powers and the full measure of their deficiencies.

Before touching upon the subject with which this chapter deals, the human pair at grips with the world of circumstance, it is only natural to make mention of Gibbon to whose authority Hardy frequently appealed in the course of his work,[2] and who, moreover, must have exerted a very definite influence upon his anti-religious thought.

With the seeds of death already lodged in its system the human pair is now hurled into the tempest of circumstance, where it must wander at the bidding of the winds. In Hardy's eyes the desire for harmony is a mere snare and chimera. Too many obstacles appear on the road which has to be traversed. First we see the tyrannical profile of passion. Then come the insurmountable prejudices of propriety or social habit. We have already seen these enemies at work. Now we have the obstinate com-

[1] *Histoire de la Literature Anglaise.* Hachette, p. 918.
[2] See preface to "*The Woodlanders*" and in the poems (Lausanne—In Gibbon's Old Garden. *Poems of the Past and Present.* Poems of Pilgrimage).

binations of chance. With Hardy the psychologist finally surrenders to the novelist. The *dénouement* appears as a climax dictated by events—that is to say, by material facts no less than as an outcome rendered inevitable by the characters. The source of the conclusion is external no less than internal. A gift of invention, which one must at times deplore, allows Hardy to insist upon his characters facing every trial that life can offer. This freedom of the imagination leads the writer to develop exhaustively the whole series of possible alternatives. Each in its turn appears, to assure the coming of misfortune. In building up this scheme, so ruinous to the last possibilities of happiness which might yet remain for the pair, Hardy brings into play an apparatus of extraordinarily hostile events. In life itself we never see such a combination of episodes, so nicely adjusted to produce an effect. The succession of calculated incidents could but serve his vision of things. It in no way corresponds with that all too frequently banal simplicity of episodes which marks the commonplace existence of the lover. But the invention allows the author to design more in harmony with his purpose the portrait of the human pair, so that it looms up against a dramatic background.

The freedom which Hardy allows himself in dealing with events contributes to confer the character of an epic of the flesh upon his work and upon the whole Odyssey of the pair. The spasms and the revolts of his men and women often result in nothing better than opening at their feet the grave that awaits them all. There are times when one listens for the sardonic laugh of a Mephistopheles at the spectacle of this progress to the abyss.

Hardy picked up his numerous incidents of intrigue in some old shop of long disused theatrical accessories, a clandestine marriage, the non-arrival of a letter, a woman's secret, the return of someone who has disappeared, the criminal action of a traitor. Such are the favourite expedients to which he constantly has recourse. Thus the letter which has not been delivered or has not been seen appears in *The Return of the Native*, *A Laodicean*, *The Mayor of Casterbridge* and *Tess of the d'Urbervilles*.

This studied complicity of events and circumstances is completed by yet other traits, which add to the strength of the laws of fatality and of psychological and moral determinism. The very atmosphere in which the drama is played moves in unison with the whole concert. On the farm at Talbothays, for instance, nature becomes tense with the mounting exhilaration of love. The pair is surrounded by a skilfully devised erotic complicity in things themselves that brings the intoxication to its climax. The god of love appears in an almost Pantheistic form and Nature herself becomes a veritable mood of love. Dogstar heat seems to hold the farm within its sway only to ripen the fruits of the earth and to bring exasperated desire to the bursting point. In *The Return of the Native* Egdon Heath constitutes a sort of active entity, composed of cosmic elements. With the singer of Wessex Destiny is a two-headed deity. It is compounded of events which sweep individuals along and of the human character which subjects each individual to his proper discipline. As Hardy grew in the mastery of his art, the psychological element triumphed over the crude fact. The interval between *Desperate Remedies*, a fit rival of certain detective stories, and *Tess*, the simple history of a pure woman, measure for us the whole extent of the tract over which he had travelled.

Thus the events, the characters and even the atmosphere of the drama bow to the author's will. Yet Hardy is too self-conscious an artist to have worked in this way without fully realising it.[1] Did he not place as a motto under the title of *Desperate Remedies* these lines of Sir Walter Scott: " Though an unconnected course of adventure is what most frequently occurs in nature, yet the province of the romance writer being artificial, there is more required from him than a mere compliance with the simplicity of reality."

If first and foremost we turn our attention to external influence, the skill with which Hardy handles events is consummate. In all the novels, above all in those which marked the beginning of his career, it expressed the art of combining coincidences, the strokes of fate and misfortune. A single example will suffice to show that with this writer realism gives way before a most fertile dramatic temperament.

In *The Mayor of Casterbridge* the novelist shows us among other scenes the defeat of Lucetta's attempts to reach happiness. Compromised by Michael Henchard, the young woman thinks she will be able to secure herself a husband in him. But the wealthy corn-dealer of Casterbridge has just encountered the woman whom he had formerly abandoned and

---

1 Hardy was not unwilling to write upon his art. In addition to his prefaces, which often reveal his ideas upon this subject, he published three review articles: " The Profitable Reading of Fiction " (The Forum, March 1888), " Candour in English Fiction (New Review, January 1890), " The Science of Fiction " (New Review, April 1891).

even sold for money to another man in a moment
of hideous aberration. The wish to atone for the
early wrongs of which he was guilty compels him to
commit a new act of injustice, to break with Lucetta
who has given herself to him. The Mayor calls upon
Farfrae, his partner, to draw up for him a letter
signifying rupture, not disclosing the name of the
recipient. The letter goes, carrying a large sum of
money, but is not delivered. The wheel turns and
Farfrae, yesterday Henchard's partner, takes the
mayor's place. A successful rival in business, the
Scotsman also becomes his rival in love for Lucetta,
and in this field, too, he is triumphant. Lucetta's
former lover embarks upon a fierce commercial
struggle hoping to get rid of his opponent. The
speculations which the mayor pursues soon impair
his position. At this moment Henchard sees in
Lucetta, who has become rich through an inherit-
ance, the wife whose fortune can save him from
disaster. How shall he constrain her to such a
marriage? By means of blackmail, threatening to
expose her past? The young woman accepts, at
least to all appearance. But she secretly becomes
Farfrae's wife. Haven is, however, not yet reached.
Hard hit by circumstances, Henchard needs Lucetta's
aid to induce his principal creditor to have patience
with him. He goes to meet the heroine. He even
saves her life in an accident, but it is only to learn
that he has saved the wife of his rival. And yet the
old merchant does not avenge himself. Is not
Lucetta's happiness then assured?

Henchard sends back to the woman who was once
his mistress the passionate letters of those past days.
His messenger opens the packet and at the " Stone

Finger " divulges the secret. The audience chuckles
over it.   Presently a procession is formed, the
habitués of the inn conceiving the idea of reviving
an old custom of escorting round the town images
of the guilty pair, Henchard and Lucetta. At the
sight of this exhibition, at once grotesque and de-
grading,[1] and at the thought of the scandal which
may ruin her happiness, Lucetta falls fainting to the
ground. She is with child and dies a few hours after.

Such is the lot of Lucetta in this novel, rich, moreover, in matter derived from several other intrigues.
The fate of Henchard is even worse in its bitterness.
He, too, goes down, this rough and brutal fighter,
overwhelmed beneath the repeated assaults hurled
against him by destiny.

What efforts the novelist put forth, all directed
against the single pair, Lucetta and Farfrae! If
dramatic qualities of a high order did not at every
point raise the value of this procedure, we should
run the risk of falling into an intrigue, recalling the
kitchen type of popular novel. A remarkable
skill is needed to uphold such a wager without
disaster. Yet the truth is that the more deeply he
sinks into the mire of difficulties, the nearer Hardy
approaches his artistic and psychological goal. At
the moment when ridicule seems to threaten, the
writer surpasses himself just by virtue of the paradoxical and exaggerated character of the situation
which he creates. Thus, in the succession of situations which he calls into being as if at will for his characters, the novelist finally exhausts the cycle of evil
possibilities, allied with the disturbing hostility immanent in things. He is for ever measuring his

1 " Skimmity ride."

heroes against an adversity which only lays down its arms in the presence of death. What saves Hardy in the excess of his intrigues is the same element which secured the Greek tragedians in the integrity of their mastery, the exactness, the more than human truth of the characters and the fidelity of their psychology to a rigorously conceived prototype. The events seem barely credible, but the characters remain kneaded out of concrete humanity broadened and simplified as the theme demands. If they are not constructed upon the same scale as ourselves, they none the less remain kinsmen, kinsmen of our hearts and of our compassion.

In consequence the human pair which he presents is magnified and, one might add, verified down to its most minute details by the trials which fate dispenses with so liberal a hand. Those whom chance attraction has brought together will find nothing but incompatibility and evil spells in the experience of marriage, and a moment comes when the co-operation of all these obstacles to marriage, sometimes trifling, sometimes formidable, always striking, renders the catastrophe inevitable.

In the same novel, *The Return of the Native*, side by side with the imperfect pair, Clym and Eustacia, we behold other victims of mischance, the yet more imperfect pair, the simple Thomasin and Wildeve. These two couples, neighbouring and akin to one another, succumb beneath a combination of blows.

In *Tess of the d'Urbervilles* and *Jude the Obscure* one might in the same way point to the movements of a cycle of material and psychological sufferings and potentialities. With a cruel irony and insistence love is several times torn from the predatory talons only to be given back to them, and we cannot hear Alec's sarcastic words without a shudder : " Remember, my lady, I was your master once : I will be your master again. If you are any man's life you are mine."

Thus one might apply to the oscillations of the mighty pendulum of destiny, which in turn bears Jude and Tess into the arms of Arabella and Sue, Alexander and Angel, the profound saying of Hardy : " So do the flux and reflux, the rhythm of change, alternate and persist in everything under the sky." Proud and bitter words in which the author sums up on his own account the thought which Shakespeare places in the mouth of Gloucester in *King Lear* :

> " As flies to wanton boys are we to the gods,
>   They kill us for their sport."

Momentous words which Hardy paraphrased in the lines with which the sorrowful history of Tess is concluded : " Justice was done, and the President of the Immortals, in Eschylean phrase, had ended his sport with Tess." " What a sport for heaven this woman Eustacia was ! " we read in *The Return of the Native*, a book in which the woman is no less harshly treated by life.[1]

Everywhere then we see the same coalition of evil forces envenoming the conflict. Everywhere love falls overwhelmed by prejudice or convention, as in the stories of Tess and Jude. In virtue of this atmosphere of tragedy there comes a moment when Hardy

---

[1] These quotations should be compared with the words uttered in one of the last scenes of " *The Dynasts* " by the Spirit of the Years, expressing in a Latin apothegm the tragic morality of the whole Napoleonic epic terminated by Waterloo, " Sic diis immortalibus placet."

no longer studies any particular pair, but the human pair in general, suddenly exalted and set free from all transitory influences. In the same way in certain moments he no longer sees in Tess the little milkmaid of Talbothays, but the very essence of the complete woman. " She was no longer the milkmaid, but a visionary essence of woman—a whole sex condensed into one typical form." Similarly in his poems, behind the infinite multiplicity of facts which might appear purely incidental, Hardy arrives at the discovery of a unity of life and an essential permanence of things.

Such is the conclusion of all these material or psychological convergences, a conclusion which is often pathetic. The stage on which the human marionettes are exhibited is controlled by an ungentle hand which does not hesitate to intervene after the fashion of a " Deus ex machina," sometimes emulating the gods of Olympus in its sport with these dolls, as it points the way for Eustacia and Tess. Hardy's drama unites with or completes the play of the gods or of the Immanent Will, the murderous activity of which he has many times discovered and denounced.[1] We ourselves behold the clash of forces which are often Protean and which are not always distinguishable from the author himself. It might, therefore, be said that this skilful staging which summons events to the rescue and which subordinates the setting to the action made Hardy a great artist or, better expressed, a creator in the full sense of the term. At times we certainly meet with excess or exaggeration. But the full effect

[1] See " The Dynasts," in which he compares this Will to a knitting-woman who has fallen asleep and whose fingers still run on in their habitual distraction.

can only be judged, if we contemplate in its perspective of human silhouettes, set off against a vast background of varied sites, the whole work of the *Wessex Novels.*

Hardy's attitude makes one think of Aeolus, resting upon the skins, wherein are imprisoned the hurricanes which let loose the tempest upon the Ocean.

As Mr Lascelles Abercrombie has shown in his study on Hardy,[1] the real cause of tragedy in life is much less the conspiracy of circumstances than man's resistance to this current of necessity, against which he strives to swim. Drama is born of this rebellion. Moreover, the struggle is from the very outset an unequal one. Need it be recalled that Hardy did not bathe his characters in any stream which rendered them indestructible? They are indeed certain to break themselves in this duel, like a blade of steel containing a straw. For not only is every figure closely dependent upon events. They are also subjected to the despotic tutelage of their own characters. The idea of liberty itself perishes under the presence of an external force, which makes every individual the instrument of that tenacious and tormenting will.

Thus a new antinomy proclaims itself, an antinomy between our own conditions and that external world which is lacking alike in nobility of causation and in a purpose which may console.

Hardy must not be unduly reproached for the great liberties, which he has taken in manipulating events. Without these defects, which add to his power, his work would not be what it is, and the

1 *Thomas Hardy.* A critical study by Lascelles Abercrombie, 1912. Martin Secker.

very defects have contributed to endow it with its
intensity of expression. In Hardy's eyes pure veri-
similitude is no criterion of truth.[1] It does not even
bear the stamp of authenticity. There is, on the
other hand, a super-natural element in certain
sequences of events. To understand some rare collaboration of circumstances, one must be able to
perceive the activities, at once artistic and sadistic,
of a power whose propulsive force gives rise to these
repetitions of coincidence. Behind all that dis-
sembles it Hardy discovers the work of that Immanent Will untiring in the creation of incidents, all
shaped to a special end. In Greek tragedy one
forgets the legendary character of the action. Like
so many great novelists, like Balzac, to quote a single
example, Hardy does not recoil before improbability,
and therein he is right. Surely it is of little importance that the circumstances could never actually
occur, provided that the characters are true and even
too human. And there is more than that in the problem. Those who have come to close quarters with
misfortune know that its paths are dark and tor-
tuous. Some would say that it is only improbable
things that happen. In Hardy's work one may
sometimes forget the element of invention under the
impression that it is the fatal arm of destiny which
may determine such attractive forces. Mischance
reveals to us the role of contingency in the world.
This role assumes such vast proportions that for

[1] Hardy seems to give genuine credence to this co-operation on
the part of circumstance. "However, Paula still stood before the
picture which had attracted her; and this, by a coincidence common
enough in fact, though scarcely credited in chronicles, happened to
be that one of the seventeenth century portraits of which de
Stancy had studied the engraved copy at Myrtle Villa the same
morning." *A Laodicean.* Book III, Chap. II.

Hardy accident is the essence of this world without
finality.

This novelist, who strikes out with such mighty
blows at the fetishes of prejudice and convention, is
not far removed by his method of constructing his
intrigue from a generation of writers which included
Charles Reade, Wilkie Collins, and even Dickens.
With its abuse of coincidence and of other similar
forms of procedure his work is influenced by the old
school which derived its inspiration from the
picaresque novel. It, therefore, still marks an era
of transition.

But, on the other hand, whereas many of these
authors strive obstinately to show that all ends for
the best in the best of worlds, Hardy is an idealist
in the opposite sense. He eliminates all the arguments of the optimistic thesis, leaving only a world
ideally cruel, forever governed by a law fraught with
calamity.

This sentiment of an evil oppression, emanating
from the tyranny of things, hangs like a great growth
of ivy about the structure which Hardy has raised.

Often an observation issues from his pen bitterly
disputing the optimism of Wordsworth or Browning.
The Wessex singer does not believe in that goodness,
in that genius of the earth which Maeterlinck has
staged for us in *La Vie des Abeilles* and *L'Intelligence
des Fleurs*.

" Is it likely," writes Maeterlinck in *La Sagesse
et la Destinée* " that when we find so much of intelligence scattered about through life, that life
itself should give no proof of intelligence ? "

He who depicted the nuptial flight as it leaves the
hive did not, like Hardy, feel any doubts as to the

efficacy of sexual selection within those very events which form the rhythm. Nor like Hardy could he discover a deceiving and disordered spectacle, an effort which miscarries and leads to nought.

There is still another aspect of the question which demands our attention. In this world, so often shaken by the storm of events, will latent and untiring derives an implicit finality from its own indestructibility. It is often subjected to a momentary check, often destroyed in its fragile incarnations by manifold conspiracies, which time and again surrender the thing created to utter annihilation.

It seems as if moving in the darkness of a grievous blindness the will to live finally reaches the point at which it devours itself and, thus, despite that guiding finality, we arrive at an internal contradiction in this universe which can be deciphered only by thought. The reader is witness of a duel between the will to live, a form of pure will as expressed in sexual obsession, and a certain phenomenalism which bars its way to the will to live.

CHAPTER X

THE POET'S QUIVER

HARDY wrote his first verses at about the age of sixteen. He was twenty-six when with such poems as " Hap," which appeared subsequently in the *Wessex Poems*, he came forward as one of the most original poets that England had ever known. His lyrical gifts were revealed to the wider public at a much later date. When his cycle of romances was complete, he deliberately chose to return to the method of expression which had borne the echoes of his first cries of pain at the indifference of the universe.

The *Wessex Poems* appeared in 1898. Since that date the lyric poet never halted, save for a few years' interruption to publish between 1903 and 1908 the great historical and philosophical drama, *The Dynasts*.

Regarded from the point of view of sex, Hardy's poetic work contains a veritable collection of examples of the cruelties involved in the sentimental life. It is for that reason that the poet has evoked for us the image of an archer, intent on driving his shafts through the ever vulnerable heart of the human pair.

Tales of love are thickly strewn throughout the

poems. As it is studied in this part of his work, the sexual question is no longer presented in its romantic form. We see rather fugitive aspects, acute moments, most frequently phases of crisis. . . . Visions of love in the heart of battle, piercing and desperate. We are presented with a drama in the dry, hard outlines of a psychologist's sketch. Its laconic utterance gives it a force and cadence all its own. The inspiration is brief, sudden and fragmentary. The whole outline vibrates with the full force of the tension. The contour is marked out by strokes abrupt and vigorous, like flashes of lightning. Every page tells of the preoccupation to retain in all its sharpness the truth, as it reveals itself at the moment when it is surprised.

Thus many pieces become little tales of cruelty. One sees amid the shadows the ever present talon of fate, like some dire leopard, lurking in ambush. Suddenly the claw flashes like a stiletto and a rag of illusion flutters to the ground.

Some stories seem as if they were drawn from a collection of miscellaneous episodes all ending tragically,[1] and the poignancy of the details leaves behind a taste of agonising bitterness. All these tales are revealing. They illustrate the partial attitude adopted by Hardy towards human nature. He is at once a witness full of pre-conceived ideas, who has intercepted these moments, and a seer capable of conversing with those who are no more, of hearing

---

[1] Those who read the biography published by Mrs Florence Hardy shortly after the poet's death, will realise from quotations drawn from Hardy's notebooks how some single trait or incident had power to strike him with all the force of a suggestion. One can follow the whole process from the original note to the poem, which is only a sharply outlined transcription of a dry anecdote.

voices from beyond the grave. For this atheist
speaks with the dead and hears their complaints.

One may read tales of girls who have been seduced,
of girl mothers, of abortions, of unfaithful husbands,
of adulterous wives. The features of vengeance and
treachery may be studied, and the chronicles of misunderstandings and ruptures. The conclusion of
these tales of passion comes with a trenchant
brutality, to teach its saddening lesson of the egoistic
perfidy shown by human beings in these conjunc-
tures, and their indifference to others' sufferings.

Events move with greater rapidity than in the
prose chapters, the rhythm is sharper, the beat more
broken, and the outline a very skeleton.

" That's the story—You see it now. That is how
the idyll came to an end, and that is how the woman
was betrayed." The whole course is run in three
strophes. " That is all there is and it always like
that." A knife-thrust and all is over. It is in this
brief and familiar tone that the poet speaks. There
is a kind of emaciation in the expression which confers upon it an abrupt and impressive eloquence.

In these verses the daughters of Wessex are depicted as too frank to answer the call of the gentleman (*The dark-eyed gentleman*) or of the village-boy
(*The Market-girl*).[1] A baby comes, but there is no
husband for Julie-Jane or for many others (Julie-
Jane).[2] They die in childbed and all is over. What
have you to do on earth, poor girls, taken in the lime
of words, spread by such a butcher of hearts as Ralph
Blossom (One Ralph Blossom soliloquizes),[3] who has

1 *Times's Laughingstocks.*
2 *Time's Laughingstocks. A Set of Country Songs.*
3 *Time's Laughingstocks.*

brought no less than seven girls to trouble? It was in chronicle literature that Hardy found his inspiration for this lady-killer, fit mate for the wenches. The poet throws no stone at Margotas. He knows well that it is the woman who pays.

One often hears the confessions of characters pursued by some tormenting image. A grief-laden voice restores for us all the sighs of love, the sob attending separation, the divorce of souls, the hypocrisy of circumstances, the lies of the heart amid the traps of life, and the perfidious inventions of destiny.

Consider these two old people. Life has united them in marriage, in defiance of all considerations of humanity. After forty years of married life they come to end their days in the poor-house. They go, respectively to his and to her wing, he to the men's side, she to the women's. What a comfort at last! Not at all, says somebody. Why separate them? An evasion of the rule is contrived, and they are brought together again. This tale is drawn from the monologue of the old husband, frustrated of his last hope. (The Curate's Kindness, A Workhouse Irony.—*Time's Laughingstocks.*)

And this other, who suddenly sees every probability of becoming a widower at the very moment when he has just found himself again in the presence of the woman whom he loves! No, his wife has not perished in the shipwreck. It is his neighbour who is bringing his dead wife ashore: "He is free. What a pity it is not me," sighs the disappointed one to his beloved. She answers with the simplicity and absence of self-consciousness of one who adapts herself to everything and never feels regrets: " It is just the same thing, *because he has long loved me too without ceasing.*" After all one man is as good as another. (*The Two Wives.*)[1]

How many times Hardy has the sentiment of separate lives which ought to be united, to complement one another. (*At Mayfair Lodgings.*)[2]

" Ainsi nous resterons séparés dans la vie,
    Et nos coeurs et nos corps s'appelleront en vain..."[3]

The stoic Angellier is surpassed by an even more negative voice, for the universe of the poet of " *A l'Amie Perdue* " is not governed by a sick god who takes please in working harm. With Hardy it is always the fault of one or the other partner that the success of the pair is compromised. How much happiness has been let go, and often for want of a single word which might have held it back ! It is as if some bulkhead stood between the two, condemning each to a solitary existence and preventing them from ever understanding one another. One does not even see as in the famous sonnet those gestures which resemble :

" . . . des signaux, sur des écueils lointains,
    De naufragés cherchant en vain à se rejoindre,
    Et se jetant dans l'air des appels incertains."[4]

A realistic and cynical poem, *A Trampwoman's*

1 *Late Lyrics and Earlier.*
2 *Moments of Vision.*
3 Thus we shall remain separated in life,
    And our hearts and bodies will call to one another in vain."
4 " . . . the signals, set upon distant rocks,
    Of shipwrecked beings, seeking in vain to join one another,
    And sending up uncertain appeals to one another."
—" *A l'Amie Perdue.*"

Tragedy, shows us the human being as architect of his own destiny and victim of an irreparable inconsequence. Does not this dramatic story portray love as it is to be met with among the tramps of Wessex ?

In a spirit of contradiction or fancifulness chance forms pairs of beings who were not intended for one another, or sometimes even unites in the grave for their last sleep two whom life has refused to join. (*The Contretemps. A Woman's Fancy.*)[1] Everywhere goes on an unceasing game of hide and seek between two people well-adapted to each other, but compelled to flee each other.

Thus the eternal pairs are made, unmade and made again, ephemeral shapes of the same clay. Untiringly the potter sets it on the wheel, indifferent to the wreckage that lies in fragments. This alone is of moment that the vessel which emerges from his hand may become the mate of another and hold together for a brief space, and that his labour should furnish vessels in sufficient number.

The destiny of the pair is always tragic. The conditions of human life demand that. The recurrence of this tragedy is expressed in terms of horrible conciseness. Each poem becomes the tiny mausoleum whose window is shut to upon a spectacle of surly abruptness.

By virtue of his power of second sight Hardy discerns destiny through the veil of time. It is often a state of somnambulism or a dream which so mightily increases his intuition of the future. What authority his presentiment confers upon his poetry ! To it is due that impression of evil, which nothing can avert and which life will always confirm. No one

1 *Late Lyrics and Earlier.*

escapes the common lot. This theme is present throughout a poem of poignant symbolism:

HONEYMOON TIME AT AN INN

At the shiver of morning, a little before the false dawn,
    The moon was at the window-square,
  Deedily brooding in deformed decay—
  The curve hewn off her cheek as by an adze;
At the shiver of morning, a little before the false dawn,
    So the moon looked in there.

Her speechless eyeing reached across the chamber,
    Where lay two souls opprest,
  On a white lady sighing " Why am I sad ? "
  To him who sighed back " Sad, my Love, am I ! "
And speechlessly the old moon conned the chamber,
    And these two reft of rest.

While their large-pupilled vision swept the scene there,
    Nought seeming imminent,
  Something fell sheer, and crashed, and from the floor
  Lay glittering at the pair with a shattered gaze,
While their large-pupilled vision swept the scene here
    And the many-eyed thing outleant.

With a start they saw that it was an old-time pier-glass
    Which had stood on the mantel near,
  Its silvering blemished,—yes, as if worn away
  By the eyes of the countless dead who had smirked
    at it,
Ere these two ever knew that old-time pier-glass
    And its vague and vacant leer.

As he looked, his bride like a moth skimmed forth and
  kneeling
    Quick, with quivering sighs,
  Gathered the pieces under the moon's sly ray,
  Unwitting as an automaton what she did;
Till he entreated, hasting to where she was kneeling,
    " Let it stay where it lies ! "

" Long years of sorrow this means ! " breathed the lady
    As they retired. " Alas ! "
And she lifted one pale hand across her eyes.
" Don't trouble, Love; it's nothing," the bridegroom
    said.
" Long years of sorrow for us," murmured the lady,
    " Or ever this evil pass ! "

And the Spirits Ironic laughed behind the wainscot,
    And the Spirits of Pity sighed.
" It's good," said the Spirits Ironic, " to tickle their
    minds
With a portent of their wedlock's aftergrinds."
And the Spirits of Pity sighed behind the wainscot
    " It's a portent we cannot abide ! "

" More, what shall happen to prove the truth of the
    portent ? "
    —" Oh; in brief, they will fade till old,
And their loves grow numbed ere death by the cark
    of care."
—" But nought see we that asks for portents there ?
'Tis the lot of all."—" Well, no less true is a portent
    That it fits all mortal mould."[1]

How vastly such an episode differs from that of the
white first married night passed by Tess and Angel
at the house at Wellbridge, once a portion of a
manorial residence and the seat of a d'Urberville,
but still a farmhouse owing to partial demolition.
In the poem there remains nothing of that softness
which Hardy the novelist leaves even on his most
poignant pages: no shade and no freshness. Here
there is no concession to the love of raiment that may
flatter. We see only garments torn upon the

1 " Moments of Vision " and " Miscellaneous Verses," in
Collected Poems of Thomas Hardy. Macmillan & Co., London
(1920), pp. 484-485. Reproduced with the consent of Messrs
Macmillan & Co.

brambles of a path that cannot be evaded—a path
that is the bed of a torrent. No flowers grow there;
the poet encounters only rocks that inflict wounds
and wayfarers covered with bruises.

How fleeting and transitory it all is, with never a
hope of recurrence ! Not without leaving its effect
upon the constancy of lovers, the beauty of woman
passes like the splendour of roses. Love's sole ransom
becomes survival in the memory and in the heart of
those who love us. But with them our own immortality perishes. It is our second and last death.
(*She to Him.*—Her Immortality.)[1] What ennobles
love is purity of sentiment, for the poet seer is
haunted by the thought of the term which death
must one day set to it. Of death, which brings all
these things to an end, he asks but one consolation,
that his own remains may become food for the worm
which has devoured his beloved.[2]

With all his macabre pessimism Hardy can still
rise into an immaterial world and celebrate in love
the rare sentiment which is borne aloft upon the
almost celestial gift of a soul. His cruel poetry sometimes rests poised in the empyrean, that poetry which
can express in all their subtle ramifications delicacy,
nuance, tremor and reserve. Could one not fix for
all eternity the minutes which precede the return of
a loved one? There is more happiness in that
moment of waiting than in the over-real minutes of
the meeting itself. (*The Minute Before Meeting.*)[3]

It is important to take note of the parallelism
existing between the themes developed in the novels,

1 *Wessex Poems.*
2 More Love Lyrics. *Time's Laughingstocks.*
3 More Love Lyrics. *Time's Laughingstocks.*

the tales and the poems. Passages already quoted
have shown many instances of similarity. Often, as
in *Tess's Lament*, the poems simply take up some
motif occurring in one of the novels. To the inter-
pretations which run through his prose Hardy seeks
to give a different direction, borne upon the wings
of that verse, at times awkward, but firm and rustic,
a verse all his own.

The recurrence in the poems of some of the themes
which have already appeared in his prose-work suggests the presence of a kind of obsession in his mind.
This frequent return to the same subjects is certainly
the indication of much tenacity of thought.

Those who are at length reunited after all the out-
rages inflicted by life, those who come late into har-
bour and can hearken to their hopes for union are
hampered by the weight of the past and by the
oppression of memories. When the final consummation takes place, the choice falls upon the sweetness
of living side by side in a friendship perfumed by that
old love, to which the burning heat of summer was
refused. It is the subject of *Long Plighted*.[1] The
same theme occurs in some measure in two tales, *The
Waiting Supper* and *Fellow Townsmen*.

Other themes appear in Hardy, more classic and
more formal. The regrets of some timid lover no
doubt admit the presence of a species of incidental
sensibility, but this renascence of a familiar theme is
not a mere decorative festoon added to all the sentimental garlands with which we are already familiar,
and which have now been flung aside. Their pure
cornflower sincerity makes them true garlands of the
fields, which one is surprised to find blooming upon

1 *Poems of the Past and the Present.*

these moors which are so little pastoral. Thus the
poets remain tributaries of the past. Each in his own
hour takes up his appointed theme in his own manner.
(To Lyzbie Browne.)[1]

Let us return to those verses, where love lies
pierced, a silent victim, its lips pinched by deception.
His clear-sightedness reveals Hardy as an observer,
armed with particularly sensitive antennæ. A spirit
which one feels to be worthy, affectionate and palpitating with life lies hidden beneath the embossed
cuirass of the poem. Pride commands that no tale
of despair with its accompanying bitterness be made
known, except with the lofty detachment of a thinker
who has ceased to be surprised, but who repeats in
his disdain the useless lesson which brings comfort
to his soul. This taciturn spirit is no doubt incon-
solable, but it is not insensible. Its deliberate stiff-
ness holds an element of pity.

Sometimes, there filters into the poem an emotion
which no one can misinterpret. (*The Last Drive*)[2]
If the eternity of separations, if the ineffable
despotism of death reappear always to bring home
to us the sense of our own nothingness and to fill
us to the full with the realisation of our insignifi-
cance, one still has the feeling that such visions are
evoked by the presence of the most undeserved
of sorrows, and that the loss of an adored wife has
inspired these cruel and poignant tones.

Something will always remain of this love that has
been laid to rest in a shroud of silk, because his muse
is daughter of Memory.

1 *Poems of the Past and the Present.*
2 *Satires of Circumstance.*

CHAPTER XI

TOWARDS A TWILIGHT HOPE

" Life is but a monotonous game, in which one is certain to win two prizes : suffering and death. Happy the child who dies on the day on which it is born ! Happier still he who never enters the world."

OMAR KHAYYAM ROBAIYAT.[1]

" Happiness is a monstrosity; punished are those who seek for it."

FLAUBERT.
(Correspondence.)

HARDY'S philosophical disposition rendered him somewhat unfit for the task of creating an atmosphere of bliss. To use his own words, " Happiness is an occasional episode in a general drama of pain." His whole intellectual conformation was opposed to it. He does not describe or even suggest the happiness that Jude or Sue might have known during the days at Aldbrickham. He could neither have been nor have become anything but the poet of life's tragedies. In his work the conflict of the sexes is dominated by fate, just as fate overhangs the drama of the Greeks. Love is the duel rendered inevitable by a fate unrighteous or enslaved. The " eternal conflict " again rises before us, the

[1] Translated from the Persian by Franz Toussaint. Edition Piazza, p. 32.

conflict which for Vigny is carried on " at all times
and everywhere " between " man's goodness and
woman's cunning." With Hardy the result is failure,
" the tragedy of unfulfilled aims."[1]

Such catastrophes, the author declares, are due to
" the fundamental error of having based a permanent
contract on a temporary feeling, which had no necessary connection with affinities, that alone render a
life-long comradeship tolerable."[1]

It is a just judgment. Hardy lays a sure finger
upon the consequences of these hasty matches which
expose human beings to the certainty of the worst
kinds of disappointment.

The wrongs suffered by each sex must necessarily
be different in kind, in view of their own physiological
and psychological differences. The passivity of her
nature renders a woman more subject either for good
or ill to the effects of fortuitous events. Such was
eminently the case with Tess. The male characters
are, at least potentially, capable of a more constructive attitude—take the example of Clym Yeobright[2]
—but that brings us no nearer to a conclusive result.
We find submission and helpless weakness in the
woman, the spirit of revolt in the man.

This idea is of essential importance in Hardy's
work and he has twice given concrete expression to
it, almost in the same words. The mere fact of the
repetition proves how deeply it had sunk into his
mind. Elfrida explains to Stephen : " I fancy I see
the difference between me and you—between men and
women, perhaps. I am content to build happiness
on any accidental basis that may lie at hand; you

---

1 *Jude the Obscure.*
2 *The Return of the Native.*

are making a world to suit your happiness."[1] Hardy
may rightly be said to speak as a psychologist and a
moralist, and the observation just quoted meets and
goes beyond the utterances of many penetrating minds.

Beneath the hammer of his thought the precious
stones of an exemplary wisdom are shaped to give
expression to a lofty morality. Proved anew and
ranged in their proper groups, they form a fit commentary upon the experiences recorded. All reveal
the sturdiness of Hardy's grip of the problem. There
is no element of haziness in the analysis. The truth
is set forth without ambiguity or disguise.

But these truths would not be without an element
of sententiousness, if they did not appear in the guise
of eminently sensible observations let fall during a
tale, a scene or a chapter. They contribute their
own sound judgment to the dialogues and the experienced reader is deeply stirred by utterances which lay
bare the human soul, surprised in all its naiveté, and
reveal its hidden sincerity, ingenuousness and depth.

What mysteries are explained by Elfrida's words,
telling of her fears and of her forebodings, when
happiness lies before her! There is a complete
psychology of woman in the girl's answer when she
advises Stephen Smith to wait for a few hours before
speaking to Parson Swancourt of their plans of
marriage: "Because if he should object—I don't
think he will; but, if he should—we shall have a day
longer of happiness from our ignorance. . . ." Few
answers allow us to advance further into the heart

1 *A Pair of Blue Eyes*, chap. VII. With these lines should be
compared the following passage from *The Return of the Native*,
book III, chap. V:—"You are just like all women. They are
ever content to build their lives on any incidental position that
offers itself; whilst men would fain make a globe to suit them."

of woman and to measure more completely the depths of its inconsequence and weakness.

"I perceive," says Alain in one of his impressive "Propos", "distinctive features which bring the two sexes into conflict with one another, without their always knowing the reason for it. The one is affective, the other active. This has often been said, but rarely explained."

The characteristics of fancifulness, incoherence and obstinacy which we encounter in woman are due to the predominance of emotional elements in a being who has to bear the burden of pregnancy and nursing. It is these characteristics which compromise the harmonious development of the pair. In man reason with its frigid calculation leads to an exclusive egoism, further complicated by jealousy or prejudice.

Misunderstandings between married persons arise from the fact that they do not employ the same language. The one speaks with the tongue of reason, the other falls back upon sensibility. The one would have life at his command, the other is sometimes content simply to accept. Thus it is lack of mutual understanding that leads to all the spite and mistrust engendered by past disputes. After every crisis each adversary withdraws to a strategic point, a Mons Aventinus, from which pride or resentment forbids descent. Each looks to the other for the gesture which shall bring peace. Nothing irreparable need have occurred between Clym and Eustacia. Neither was free from blame. The affection that still remained between them was strong enough for the resumption of life in common, perhaps, too, upon a firmer basis.

Although the pair remains a true constitutive monad in the mechanical universe, envisaged by the novelist, its inner substance contains the leaven of hatred. The sentiments accompanying love reveal themselves by spasmodic outbursts and by acts of rebellion. Love, in short, always upholds its character of a conflict, ending in a twofold defeat, for the pair and for its champions.

Not content to profit by psychological realities, Hardy employs misfortune as a favourite accomplice in ruining all hopes and in slaying all dreams. Love, that desire for happiness which may be shared, the dream of a Jude, whose brow is haunted by thoughts of suicide, can only be the source of a constant conflict between the sexes amid the daily demands of life. A tormented genius, Hardy sees them dominated by an unending and savage antagonism, which renders all the catastrophes unavoidable.

In his book, *Le Roman Anglais Contemporain*, M. Firmin Roz speaks in the following terms of Hardy's work : " In virtue of its origin and its governing principle the passion of love involves a contradiction which must destroy it ! . . . The passion is simply egoism shared by two persons ; it is a counter-sense."[1] No happiness, then, is vouchsafed to the pair. Two beings, each aspiring solely to engulf and make an end of the other, are irrevocably opposed to one another at the very moment when they are dreaming of the perfection of happiness. Man and woman together make up an antinomy which cannot be resolved. Their dualism is opposed to a harmonious union.

One of the few pairs to find a moment's grace in Hardy's eyes is the pair formed from the union of

1 *Le Roman Anglais Contemporain.*   Hachette, 1912.

Elisabeth-Jane and Donald Farfrae. Their affection does not spring from the revelation of affinities as precarious as they are sudden. It is, on the other hand, life which gradually knits them together. The two feel sympathy and esteem for one another, so that after long experience of the conspiracies of events their well-seasoned wisdom, aided by Elisabeth's persevering goodness, suffices to triumph over the plot of destiny and to unite them. Such a victory is not accorded by life to those creatures who impulsively follow the behests of their instincts. The two young people are both sensitive to the charm which each exercises upon the other, but always within the bounds of moderation. The Scotsman's seductive powers never cloud the cool reason of Elisabeth-Jane. On the other hand, Farfrae does not at once discover in her—by one of these impassioned glances which certain heroes send forth—the inevitable companion of his life. We are told that each has for a long time hesitated before arriving at that happy compromise which consists in a combination of the good qualities of both. Thus their united efforts lay the cornerstone of their home. And one cannot doubt that it is only after all the ravages of which they have been witnesses or victims that they find their equilibrium on that line of moderation. Hardy quotes the saying of Novalis : " Character is destiny." If it sometimes happens that two persons stand out as exceptions among so many pairs doomed to the most cruel misfortune, it is because they do not allow or cease to allow themselves to be carried away by their own dispositions as by a torrent, and because they are not willing to submit to all the rigours of the law of sex.

The convergent aspirations of Elisabeth-Jane and

Farfrae are for a long time turned aside from their path by the appearance of Lucetta. She is at once subjugated by the Scotsman's frank and vibrating charm. Ambitious and sensual, she labours to communicate her own intoxication to him. Once more we see the fleshly pair yielding to the pricks of desire. And yet, notwithstanding all the vicissitudes which it has known and all the disasters which it has caused, love still retains in Hardy's eyes a profound significance and an unequalled prestige.

Aided by the intact virtue of those forces of purity and nobility which dwell within it, it sometimes crowns by a tardy but splendid act of reparation the catastrophe which has swallowed up all the errors of a lifetime.

Eustacia and Wildeve are reunited in death, like those two in *A Few Crusted Characters*. Separated by the bonds which link them with others, they perish in each other's arms at the end of a trip on the sea. Love can achieve in death what the enemy forces have forbidden during life. Betrothed in the spirit alone, it is with the shade of Giles that poor Marty is united. A living statue of devotion, she is often to be seen hanging over the premature grave of the apple-planter. When Jude dies, Arabella gives utterance to the final truth contained in that sombre book, when she says of Sue: " She's never found peace since she left his arms, and never will again till she is as he is now."[1]

---

1 This profound utterance of disillusionment is probably equally applicable to Arabella herself. Did she not also, after much suffering, return to the arms of Jude? Does one not find in these two cases a kind of echo of the theory upheld by Zola in *Madeleine Férat*, the theory of the impregnation of the woman by the man who has possessed her."

Thus it was in very truth the sexual problem, alike within and without the limits of marriage, which had been stated with such terrible frankness, sending a shudder through British sentimentality, so nicely draped in its pink and blue raiment. In the tension and pathos of the psychological situations Hardy, in spite of his apparent objectivity, fought, fairly indeed, but assuredly fought on behalf of certain ideas, sure alike of himself and of the weakness and littleness which may be found in life. The fatal contingencies, the mean prejudices and the social deceit, the tyranny of which is responsible for the tragic grandeur of more than one ending, veil a mighty labour of sincerity, which could only result in a noble effort of liberation.

In reality Hardy had all the grim sadness of the thinker and idealist. There is much to learn from his brutal sincerity and cruel frankness. They teach us that real happiness rests solely upon the full activities of will and consciousness, upon the security of truth accepted without reticence and sometimes outside the realm of convention and of the restraints which it imposes. The lofty realisation of such happiness is not pursued with sufficient tenacity by Hardy's characters. Unsatisfied at heart they are for ever led by their passions and finally become the victims of the obscure forces, the fruit of whose workings is that which cannot be undone.

The only happiness which they can reach is that precarious, but none the less real and dearly bought happiness which poor Tess knows for a brief space in the arms of Angel Clare after the liberating crime, which is soon to take her from Stonehenge to prison and to the gallows. This happiness indeed always appears in the author's eyes as a rare fruit, an unstable combination, the result of coincidences which can only take shape and dissolve amid the unbroken circle of human suffering.

More serene than Hardy, some among his contemporaries refused to accept this abdication in the face of inevitable misfortune. Panting victims of our own egoism and all its madness, shall we, they say, continue to let ourselves be guided in life solely by the force of our instincts?

Man is first and foremost a sexual animal, but his sexual impulses must be educated no less than his mind. In a sphere which is as essential to his happiness as to the reproduction of the species he must not be left a prey to the same uncertainties as those which beset the characters of Thomas Hardy.

Many, therefore, have appealed against the sentence pronounced at the end of the *Wessex Novels*. At the moment when the master of Max Gate was depicting Jude and Tess, the master of Box Hill introduced *Lord Ormont and his Aminta* to the public. With this writer optimism flowered upon the very soil which had produced the philosophy of Ibsen and Hardy. In spite of his sensitiveness and of the complex character of his intelligence Meredith finds his law of equilibrium in the respect for living reality and in the rejection of abstract concepts. The disintegrating forces of analysis do not break up the personality, and in his eyes intelligence subsists as one of the actual conditions of the individual's expansion. His heroes become a species of moral champion. His women are active, not passive. Their thought gleams like a luminous point, which attracts as much if not more than their beauty. Their rôle suggests that of a guardian angel, and a Diana Warwick is at the same time lucidly conscious of the true aim of the emancipation of women. The struggle for existence takes on the form of a struggle for the fullest possible comprehension. In the love-scenes one always hears some strain of a celestial melody. Meredith's pair does not tread its appointed path in the grip of that obscure and overwhelming power which we meet in *Jude* and in *The Return of the Native*. Amid the sheen of a dewy morning two creatures, like unto children of Eden, seem to rise up from bushes covered with gossamer, more joyously compounded for the experiences of life, to face less exacting trials in a deserted island which is none other than England.

The author's malice appears in the features of the young squire, but what admirable heroes he has chosen, to present on a background of instruction and faith the spectacle of a salutary encounter, a precious lesson!

In this pair the man and woman appear as two halves whose efforts must set free a common store of concrete, light-hearted humanity, in place of embarking upon an analytical process which over-stimulates the senses. An ardent feminist, Meredith extends a generous hand to woman that she may issue forth from the rut of centuries. He has drawn all the inevitable conclusions from the intimate tragedy of *Modern Love*, the story of a first failure in marriage. There is no road to happiness, if the eternal feminine persists in wandering amid the mazes of a purely instinctive psychology, which gives no scope to courage. While Hardy's sexual psychology is at once courageous and disillusioned, he who gave utterance to it was surrounded by the careful solicitude of the two female companions of his life. Neglected in his childhood and unhappy as a husband, Meredith seems to have risen from amid his trials with the smiling hope of a flash of sunlight following upon a storm.

With Hardy, even Ethelberta, of all his heroines the most clear-sighted in her handling of love, the only one capable of conducting an intrigue to the end which she has marked out, the heroine who avoids contact with any purely sentimental adventure, holds obsolete views upon the relations between man and woman, tainted with the old principles of coquetry and so-called feminine cunning.

Her counsels to her sister Picotee are not perhaps very edifying, but in her eyes it is a matter of little importance that the combat is not carried on with clean weapons. According to her it is for the woman to defend herself and at the same time to win the day. She instructs her younger sister in the rules of the ancient game, in which it is the grand object to keep the suitors in a state of suspense. The elder sister says to Picotee : " Men who come courting are just like bad cooks; if you are kind to them, instead of ascribing it to an exceptional courtesy on your part, they instantly set it down to their own marvellous worth."

There is then no question here, as in the novels of Mr H. G. Wells, of putting new wine into old bottles. Moreover, Ethelberta is a cool-headed creature, who, in the interests of her family, ends by marrying old Lord Mountclere. This conclusion is no apotheosis for the heroine, who has done nothing more than adroitly play her rôle of little governess who rises to the rank of peeress, without her destiny becoming an example or a source of instruction.

Ethelberta's success constitutes an exception. Hardy rarely indicates any road by which his characters may emerge from the blind alley into which he has thrust them. He seeks for no issue from the strait. In most cases he is content to swing his axe and strike the creature down. The possibility of avoiding misfortune could only lie in the adoption of a more flexible attitude. But so far from tacking about, his characters deliberately break themselves against the danger which threatens. Yet this writer, who was able to express his thoughts without the aid of huge parentheses, even without giving undue prominence to his reflections, causing them to stand out upon the substance of his novels; who lets fall allusive observations at the foot of a page or at the end of a paragraph, could not fail to see the advantages of a compromise which would safeguard the possibility of a habitable universe. He did incidentally show the merits of so pragmatic an attitude in a sentence in *Far from the Madding Crowd*,[1] and he also made it clear that there are such things as salutary concessions and that a little opportunism is better than too much rigour. The necessity of compromise, which in his own person he refused to admit, was, then, apparent to him and in a kind of accessory observation he denounced the danger of carrying the reasoning process to its final stage. A more wavering line of conduct would have saved

---

1 " . . . . the untoward fate which so often attends dogs and other philosophers who follow out a train of reasoning to its logical conclusion and attempt perfectly consistent conduct in a world made up so largely of compromise."

Hardy's characters from provoking adversity, and
the story of the pair would not have been marked by
such miserable issues.

In the opinion of Wells, the obsessing and fundamental problem of sexual relations must, if possible,
receive a social solution. That, he holds, would be
most surely attained by a complete revision of our
conception of woman and by summoning the latter
to modify her attitude towards man. Wells calls for
the adoption of a definite line of policy towards the
sexual question.

Realising the extent to which the problem dominates all other problems and that in social life
reproduction takes precedence over production, the
author of *Joan and Peter* could only approach the
subject with courage and decision. He sees the
reality and depicts the torments of sex, showing us
the young men whose work it disturbs. As M.
Georges Connes says in his book, *La Pensée de Wells*,
" his heroes are victims of Dame Nature." But, unlike Hardy, Wells has a constructive mind. His eye
is on the future. He would make of woman, the
chosen of man, his associate in citizenship, his companion in the fullest sense, no longer the victim of
an out-of-date orientalism. What, then, this great
originator of ideas and theories seeks, is the elevation
of woman; the disappearance of the eternal Delilah
and of the nice little animal. It is for this that the
iconoclast of obsolete idols calls. The nuptial flight
which Wells envisages as a possibility, once the law
of healthy selection is in operation, is unknown in
Hardy's work. Written in 1909 in the thick of the
Feminist agitation for the acquisition of the vote,
Anne Veronica is audacious to the point of paradox.

On the woman's part it shows us a masterfulness which allows her to forsake the free union imposed upon love by legal obstacles, to reach land none the less in the haven of marriage. This free gift, which most commonly leads to shame and desertion, in this case shows the way to the most harmonious realisation of the pair, triumphant over ignorance and vice. The future is assured when a real selection has united in the pair love and almost fraternal affection, which must become its corollary and its safeguard. This act of faith makes us think of some of Meredith's heroines and even of Shakespeare's Portia.

It really seems as if a whole literature had sprung into existence, to embrace all the problems connected with marriage and divorce or to examine them with new and modern eyes.

In *Erewhon* and *The Way of all Flesh*, Samuel Butler satirised bourgeois sexual morality and exposed the fiasco of the prejudices.

Mr Havelock Ellis has compelled sympathetic understanding of a world long veiled beneath taboo by his noble pages of propaganda and his scientific investigation of the facts of sex. He has secured for sexual intercourse an interest similar to that attending upon the procreation of fruits and insects. The Irish humorist, Bernard Shaw, the lively Socialist, has written plays (*You never can tell. Man and Superman. Getting married. Heartbreak House.*) wherein he has shown how difficult it is to escape from the old formulae which he finds detestable, whence it would appear that on this secular ground innovations are dangerous and sometimes puerile. The biting satire and the firework display of paradoxes do not avail to disguise the fact that the well-trodden paths are still more sure than the faintly indicated short cuts. His heroes, indeed, are not a whit the less eloquent in speaking of the constraints and servitude implied in definite engagements. They are conscious of the omnipotence of sexual attraction within the strategic framework of the duel of the sexes. But they know how to avoid falling under its sway and can resume possession of themselves.

Hardy, in his solitude, only looked at certain aspects of the problem and these he always beheld through spectacles tinted with pessimism. We do not hear, as with Wells, the strains of the nuptial hymn. The curtain descends upon a finale of tragedy, revealing the noble despair of a thinker, whose epilogues one is fain to close with this lapidary phrase : " Man must not be the slave of man."

Thus we are faced with a dilemma. For unless this death-bearing robe of Nessus be laid aside by a constant effort of will, life has nothing to offer to the unhappy beings, who are for ever questioning themselves, but useless and painful trials. One recalls the terrible utterance in *The Dynasts* of one of the Phantom Intelligences, whose voices are heard throughout the epic. The Spirit cries out at the spectacle of the sufferings imposed upon poor mortals :

> " A juster wisdom his who should have ruled,
> They had not been."[1]

An apology for non-existence, such, too, is the conclusion appended by Hardy to *Jude the Obscure*, as by Ibsen to the final scene of *Hedda Gabler* and

[1] *The Dynasts*, act I, scene 11. Compare the phrase of Schopenhauer : " If a God exists, I would not be in his place. The spectacle of the world's misery would break my heart."

by Wagner even to the closing measures of *Götter-dämmerung*.

To produce this effect the writer summons a very strange figure whom he makes his spokesman. The son of Jude and Arabella, " Father Time ", exhales a precocious breath of the will to suicide. The child is sickly and prematurely aged, the last of a line, every member of which has been cast up upon the shores of life, a wreck. " Why," it says in effect to its new mother, who is Sue, " Why are you going to have another child, when it is already beyond your power to feed us ? " Why, indeed ? And the child itself will draw the right inference, in dragging after it to death the two younger children. The following morning on coming back to the lodgings with Jude, Sue finds the three children hanging from two pegs and from a nail. Thus " Father Time " commits the criminal act and sacrifices himself with the children, because they are too numerous. In Hardy's eyes those heroes who incarnate the disgust for life are forerunners. They are the chance emissaries, coming in advance of the more highly developed generations which will definitely incarnate the as yet sporadic desire not to raise up seed. Such are already Jude and Sue and Tess, and even Clym in *The Return of the Native*. For this writer as for Schopenhauer, to elude the desire to live is to give proof of a deeper knowledge of the real nature of life ! It is the sign whereby one may recognise the ultimate triumph of liberty over the horrible misery of existence, the victory of intelligence over the Immanent Will. This superior attitude is akin to asceticism in its neutrality and its doctrine of renunciation.

After Leopardi, Schopenhauer, von Hartmann,

Leconte de Lisle and Madame Ackermann, Hardy
questions himself regarding the purpose of existence
and finds his answer in these terms of negation. As
we have already read in the story of Tess, children
are called into existence without any desire on their
part, as a mere consequence of an act of love. And
the parents who create these beings condemn them
to share in their own misfortunes. The last redeem-
ing hope, which might still exist for the pair, is dis-
solved in the bitterness of the final drop of sediment.
For the fleshly pair by creating life becomes responsible for a fundamental and organic act of injustice. The writer shows how criminal it is to bring
beings into the world, if it entails exposing them to
conditions of misery and desertion. Duty lies in
begetting no children at all when the cradles do not
enjoy a minimum of decency and security, so that
human dignity may be preserved. Through the
conscience of Tess, Hardy blames the parents who in
their carelessness continue to produce children and
to compromise by new arrivals the already ill-assured
position of the earlier born. A problem of the utmost
gravity this, deriving its original inspiration from
Malthus.

It was not for the first time that this cry of doubt,
and surely, too, of despair, was heard. The throat
of Lucretius had already burnt with the same thirst
for annihilation. The *De Rerum Naturâ* shines from
afar like some mighty ancestor of the *Wessex Novels*
and of the *Dynasts*. Each writer in his atheism can
give the hand to the other. They offer other analogies
by their conception of a purely mechanical universe.
Thus, working nought but injustice and destruction,
life is not worth living.

" Tu quidem ut es leto sopitus, sic eris aevi
    Quod superest cunctis privatus doloribus aegris."
                              (904-905.)

" Cur non ut plenus vitae conviva recedis
    Aequo animoque capis securam, stulte, quietem ? "
                              (938-939.)
                            LUCRETIUS, III.[1]

Yet over and over again, and not only in his de-
clining years, Hardy threw off the yoke of negation.
He beheld the possibility of liberation for this enslaved world. He saw it obscurely tracing itself a
path which should lead to the next stage.

Sometimes it was as if a dove flew forth from this
pessimism, so lightly borne by the lean old countryman, towards some distant ark of hope.

> " Yea, on, near the end,
>   Its doings may mend;
>   Aye, when you're forgotten,
>   And old cults are rotten,
>   And bulky codes shotten,
>
>   XENOPHANES ! "[2]

A work of imagination or sensibility is rarely well
adapted as a vehicle for the expression of doctrine.
Whoever sets out with the definite intention of in-
terpolating maxims or speculations in a novel or
poem is steering straight for the rocks. Didactics are
always tedious and utilitarian, and pure research can

[1] " And thou, thou shalt remain until the end of time even as
thou art in the slumber of death, exempt from all suffering and
toil."
    " Why, then, guest that hast eaten and drunk thy fill, why not
withdraw from the table of life? Why, poor fool, not accept with
serenity a rest which nothing will disturb? "
[2] Xenophanes, the monist of Colophon. *Human Shows.*

only be carried on in an atmosphere purged of all possible contagion.

But a work realised without any hidden philosophical, metaphysical or psychological purport may yet naturally hold within itself some such implication, forming a true part of its own substance. In that case creation will find a basis of matchless excellence in such a thought that knows every phase of the drama of man's questioning and exploration.

It is doubtless due to the fact that it instinctively approaches these problems of transcendant importance, bending upon them a gaze the courage of which is only equalled by its lucidity, that Hardy's work touches nothing which it does not clothe with an august beauty. And always we hear the murmurs of all the refusals of a conscience which forbids itself any weakness.

It was Hardy's genuine and sincere claim to write stories and it is by the range of these stories that the worth of his work may be estimated.

In place of a series of etiolated intrigues and thread-bare adventures we have ample silhouettes limned directly from the life, presenting the passionate and sorrowful image of a humanity, enslaved to its destiny, but ever thwarted in its purpose. And the whole symbolism of the pair contains the epitome of a world even vaster and no less mysterious.

CHAPTER XII

HARDY'S KINGDOM

THIS is perhaps the moment for leaving the flesh and all its torments and turning to an aspect of Hardy which some of his readers prefer above all others.

In Wessex, the legendary kingdom bequeathed by Alfred, where almost all his scenes are laid, Hardy was king.

He was the unchallenged monarch of the counties of Berkshire, Wiltshire, Somerset, Hampshire, Dorset and Devon, united under the sceptre of his pen. What authority he wielded in a country which owed to him the revelation of its beauty!

It was only at a later stage that his work rose to the heights of that metaphysical vision and thought which confers upon it a place among the greatest works of art. Yet, before becoming the modern classical tragedy of sex, what he created is, to begin with, a state of sensibility affecting the sight, the smell and the hearing. It is the panorama of those grass-grown, leafy pasture-lands. It is the scent of the orchard in October, the creamy odour around the apple-trees hard by the dairies, the fragrance of cut hay on the banks of the river in June. It carries to us the chants of all the trees, the hermits of the heath and the chorus of the forest. With a

184

record of sensory observations of astonishing scope, it interprets the whispering of the wind upon every species of leaf. What treasures ignored by our eyes and lost to our ears, to our sense of smell and even to our touch have thus been preserved from oblivion!

Spontaneous renown is the due of first-rate descriptive powers. If Berri owes its romantic immortality to George Sand, if George Eliot has revealed an unknown Warwickshire, if the Polish countryside is now inseparable from Ladislas Reymont, if Selma Lagerlöf has brought poetry to Veermland, Wessex owes to Hardy its fairest title of nobility.

It must not be supposed that the writer inhabited a region with which none could compare in beauty, or that such spots exist nowhere else. What is true is that all these landscapes of meadow and wood, all these pictures of villages and rustic scenes are indebted for their existence to Hardy. This wonderful observer discovered things that did not exist for the ordinary eye. It is enough to travel in Wessex to be convinced that many a land may become a realm charged with poetry and beauty, if only it finds the hand which will illuminate it.

What Hardy did for his little country was a work of piety, emotion and love no less than of genius. It is inspired by all the grandeur that can spring from the exaltation of the soil. A great painter can always achieve with the head of a peasant woman a canvas worthy of a Rembrandt or a Holbein.

Hardy is great in virtue of his penetrating and flexible interpretation of his native earth. He could see quartz crystals amid the pebbles, and each object stood before him in unique and striking outline.

With the appearance of that faculty for imparting

his impressions and memories and for ranging the play of lights and colours in these pastoral scenes the kingship of the master was assured and his kingdom laid under the spell of the miracle of resurrection.

Before the great Exhibition of 1851 and the appearance of the railway, these counties led a sequestered existence amid their own customs, and Hardy witnessed the decline of those practices which safeguarded the personality of country-life, and which to-day make up its legend. With their expiring sigh he received their spirit.

Hardy was not one of those for whom the manifestations of collective life remain a forbidden land. His conclaves of peasants offer a humorous assemblage of types curious and even droll, at the same time exhibiting their shrewdness; a whole social fauna of a past age. One recalls the inimitable rustics of Shakespeare's theatre in the presence of these simple beings with their dialect talk, creatures of a humanity, fashioned according to the rhythm of the seasons. Just as fierce warriors started up from the teeth of the dragon slain by Cadmus, so they, too, seem to have emerged from a tree-trunk or from the clay covered by the green fleece of the meadows, these worthies so well versed in Nature's ways, so closely associated with that earth which nourishes them and supports them upon her bosom.

No work was more closely conditioned by its geographical co-ordinates. No writer was less free from their grip. Hardy left his native earth only to rise to the plane of metaphysics, where all visions of Nature are polarized.

The epic poem of *The Dynasts* adds to this

profound and many-sided work the monumental
proportions of a completed structure, in which the
spaciousness of the situations and the thunder of an
astounding cosmogony outgo any theatrical element
in the action, leaving us before a world subject to
unfathomable and inexorable laws.

Little adapted to our range of vision, this mighty
work may even repel by the anachronism of its
machinery. And yet what a gain to the philosophy
of history! Everything in the spectacle is both
enlarged and diminished, enlarged by the terrifying
participation of the Immanent Will, diminished by
the abasement of the characters reduced to the rôle
of playthings in the Hand of Destiny.

Over this aspect of his work is laid the alluvial
soil of the poems, coming in successive strata to proclaim the poet's detachment regarding whatsoever
there be of joy to the eye or enchantment of grove
and forest in his cycle of romance.

They bear the stigma of manifold experiences.
The rain of blows directed as upon the same tortured
anatomy is unceasing and impenetrable. In his pre-
science and lucidity the poet does not omit to note
a single bruise.

It would seem that in growing old the gnarled oak
of the Forest of Wessex put forth branches rather
than foliage, and that the green boughs remained
near the soil. The top is bare, upright and obstinate.
It towers aloft, pointing like a forefinger to heaven.

APPENDICES

APPENDIX I

NOTE ON FREUD AND HARDY

" A dream of mine flew over the mead
To the halls where my old Love reigns."
" The Dream Follower."

Poems of the Past and the Present.

FUTURE historians will find it very difficult to assign limits to the inroads of Freudianism. Is there a single psychologist of love whose work does not show traces of it? The domain of psycho-analysis is at once vague and full of variety. No far-reaching investigation, no statement of moment can be entirely divorced from it. Psycho-analysis may help us to understand Hamlet, Lady Macbeth, Doctor Faustus or Julien Sorel.

Translations of Freud, however, appeared in England too late for it to be at all likely that the Viennese professor could have exercised any influence upon Hardy's thought. The first English translations of Freud date from 1909. Scientific literature dealing with his work became popular about 1917. It was crowned by the appearance in 1920 of *Introductory Lectures to Psycho-Analysis.*

It would no doubt be a futile task to look for any

close and literal correlation between Freud and Hardy. It would even be an anachronism at the moment when a lively reaction is setting in against these theories. But we should be passing over a point of material importance, if we failed to show that the doctrines of the Austrian psychologist are in no respect at variance with anything in the Wessex cycle. Though he would condemn me for saying it, Hardy was a Freudian before Freud.

Obsession with the problem of sex is the outstanding trait common to both. Freud and Hardy saw in love the great psychical and biological motive force in the midst of a world, in which the unconscious is the larger circle, containing the narrower circle of conscious life.

In what respect are Hardy's characters Freudian? However prompt many of his heroes are in their response to the challenge of sex, once the passion is revealed, its manifestations are compelled by the pressure of circumstances to disappear. Its victim must then force it back within him. We have seen the tyranny exerted by these emotions, repressed and almost stored up, in the cases of Tess, of Elfride and of many other women. What outlet will be found after this process of voluntary inhibition? Repression only delays the discharge, and the consequences of the delay are deplorable.

May not the dream, as with Freud, at times become the unconscious and symbolic expansion of a psychological repression?

By what method should we seek to interpret dreams? A complete revolution in our explanation of them is involved, if we conceive of them as gushing forth like water, bursting the pipes when the

pressure is too strong. Repressed love feels the need
for manifesting and realising itself. Another mode
of expression becomes necessary.

No book of dreams is needed to interpret the
vision of Stephen Smith in the train which carries
himself and Knight, and to which is attached the
mortuary-coach of Elfride, whom both men love.
Neither knows that she is dead. They have set out,
each upon the same errand, to recover the first place
in her affections. With Freud as with Hardy, the
dream is symbolical. In this novel, *A Pair of Blue
Eyes*, he makes a presentiment his starting point.
At first unaccountable, this dream is clearly the pro-
longation of an unconscious thought. After imposing
a censorship upon his love, Smith can see evil omens
on all sides. Their interpretation is clear and they
are already realised.

In Hardy's eyes there exists a connection between
dream and reality, endowed with power to transform
something that is desired into concrete actuality, as
in that tale of Wessex, entitled *The Withered Arm*,
where the substance of a dream is imprinted upon
the flesh of a woman.

In *A Group of Noble Ladies* the story of Annetta[1]
illustrates the attention which Hardy bestowed upon
all psychical cases. A young woman who has come
by the process of crystallization to love a young
nobleman admits on her deathbed having given birth
to an illegitimate child. There is absolutely no truth
in her statement, and, moreover, adultery with the
young lord was materially impossible at the moment
when the child was conceived. It is an instance of
repressed love which yearns to have created some-

1 Squire Petrick's Lady.

thing. Illusion sweeps aside the truth and usurps
its place.

Hardy delights in all these symptoms, believing
in the frequency of their occurrence. He accepts
pathological cases without any incredulity.

After the scene at the mill at Wellbridge, in which
Tess reveals to him her secret, the single failure in
her life, Angel gets up at night in a sleep-walker's
dream. He imagines his wife to be dead; and indeed
to him she is morally dead. Such is the symbolism
of the trance. Then he takes the trembling Tess in
his arms and seeks to bury her in a sarcophagus.
The next day there is no trace of the automatism
and no sign of the dreamer's distress beneath the
prejudices which are working towards a separation.[1]

But it is more especially the heroes of the poems
who are invested with a kind of psychic aura. They
may truly be said to emit invisible waves, differing
specifically from those which determine the action
of the characters charged with sexual emotions in
the novels.

The poet frequently has recourse to states of hallucination, in which the subject, stricken with a
veritable catalepsy of the consciousness, lives again
through a whole period of his repressed mental
life.[2]

The characters move in an atmosphere of physical
life so intense that there is an incessant confusion
between dream and reality.[3] They are neurotics,
accustomed to the evocation of phantoms.[4]

[1] *Tess of the d'Urbervilles,* chap. XXXVII.
[2] The Revisitation, *Wessex Poems.* The Re-enactment, *Satires
of Circumstances.* The Glimpse, *Moments of Vision.*
[3] A dream or not. *Time's Laughingstocks.*
[4] After a journey.

But there can be no doubt that the Freudian analysis throws a powerful light upon the underworld of sexual life and of the conflict of the sexes. In Hardy's work we encounter the " libido ", that manifestation of all the instincts connected with sex. There is no real opposition between such a passage as the following and many pages in the work of the novelist and poet which have attracted our attention : ". . . the sexual function is the only function of a living organism which extends beyond the individual and secures its connection with its species. It is undeniable that the exercise of this function does not always bring advantage to the individual, as do his other activities, but that for the sake of an exceptionally high degree of pleasure he is involved by this function in dangers which jeopardize his life and often enough exact it. Quite peculiar metabolic processes, different from all others, are probably required in order to preserve a portion of the individual's life as a disposition for posterity. And finally the individual organism that regards itself as first in importance and its sexuality as a means like any other to its own satisfaction is from a biological point of view only an episode in a series of generations, a short-lived appendage to a germplasm which is endowed with virtual immortality, comparable to the temporary holder of an entail that will survive his death."[1]

The full significance of many observations scattered throughout the works of many an author reveals itself to those who are acquainted with the writings of Freud and of his disciples. A knowledge

[1] *Introductory Lectures on Psycho-Analysis.* Twenty-Sixth Lecture, p. 345. Authorised English translation by Joan Riviere.

of psycho-analysis confers upon them more value and a wider scope.[1]

Psycho-analysis, then, can offer a method of investigation, rich in possibilities for the criticism of the phenomena of the life of the soul and of the unconscious. With its aid we shall be better equipped for understanding abnormal characters and even for explaining them.

Herein lies the justification of the success enjoyed by Freudian doctrines in the world of letters.

1 " Narcissism," the adoration of self appears in the egoism of which Angel and Knight are very representative examples.

APPENDIX II

A VISIT TO THOMAS HARDY

AFTER leaving Waterloo Station the train glides away from London towards Southampton and Dorchester. The pilgrim who is about to apply the test of reality to the images traced by the *Wessex Novels* of that land where the Hardyan cycle runs its course, examines his memories with every change in the landscape, bidding them recognise their own features in the nature through which he travels. Green valleys, girdled with clumps of trees, wild stretches of country, covered with gorse and scanty fringes of ancient beeches, seem to press about the window like the still imperfectly identified originals of the scenery, amid which all these tragedies of the soil were enacted.

As commonplace as one could wish, the little station of Dorchester is excellently adapted to sweep away all the prestige of art. But sadness is not lacking and one thinks of some of Hardy's poems, such as *On the departure platform*.[1] And yet when one is suddenly confronted with the enormous red wall of the brewery, there is a strong temptation to regard Hardy as an imposter. Is this really Casterbridge ?

[1] *Time's Laughingstocks.*

A hotel omnibus meets the travellers and at last memory is stirred at the sight of the cattle-pens all ready for market-day. To-day everything is deserted, but we see the osier hurdles waiting to confine the sheep, no doubt branded in red. Where are you, Diggory Venn, Gabriel Oak? Perhaps you have left for Puddletown (Weatherbury)?

At Dorchester one should stay at the " King's Arms." Indeed there is nowhere else to stay, if one would become more closely acquainted with the spirit of the place and understand how Hardy's creative work took its rise with the spatial character of his inspiration. Set amid its musical bells the " King's Arms " is a solid, old-fashioned English inn. With its columned porch standing out upon the street, it must be at least a century old. The sporting and racing prints which adorn the passages and staircases tell of that fabled world of joviality and " country-life " upon which they have looked down.

The " King's Arms " is almost a character in Hardy's work. In *The Mayor of Casterbridge* Henchard entertains the dignitaries of the town at the " King's Arms ", while from the steps on the other side of the street Mrs Newson and her daughter try to distinguish their " relative." Surely these walls will revive for us the life of those characters and even reveal the existence of all those rustics who came on fair-days to stuff themselves with food and beer. What Pickwickian travellers have not snored through heavy siestas in the " lounge " upstairs, where the famous banquet was held? At the " King's Arms " one can easily imagine the arrival of the stage-coach and of the travellers on horseback, all that picturesque world preserved for us by Washing-

ton Irving, and a whole tempting literature of good
cheer and blazing logs.

In Dorchester (Casterbridge) one is impressed at
every step with the freedom and fidelity with which
the writer used his models.   This is equally true for
the two bridges crossing the river below the town
where we find the failures, those defeated by life,
who always come to stroll there; for the upper part
of the town or for " Colyton House ", which suggested some of the features of Lucetta's abode.
" Colyton House " looks on to a narrow street, which
does not command the market-place, but the key-
stone may be seen with its grimacing and symbolical
mask.

Hardy built his house near the town, upon a ridge
from which the outlines of a simple landscape seem
to slope down and meet.   One crosses the cutting
where the detested railway has set up its kingdom.
The tarred road pursues its way towards hamlets,
farms, manor-houses and other towns.   Then there is
a short wall running like a girdle round a mass of
green.   A gate near which one reads the words " Max
Gate " shows the way to the hermit's abode.

A broad and winding avenue leads to the house.
Somewhat Dutch in its outline of red bricks, the
house was constructed according to the plans of Mr
Hardy, architect.   It was no doubt his dream to
possess this retreat in the heart of the country of
which he will for ever bear the keys, the keys of
romance, of enchantment, and of vision.

Is Mr Hardy at home ?   The door is closed to the
entreaties of strangers, to eager journalists, to bands
of Americans, and to the indiscreet, itching for auto-
graphs.   Such are the orders at Max Gate.   The

author of *The Return of the Native* has no desire to
figure in the comedy of glory. For him it is enough
to be read. He holds that to look upon him can have
no virtue for the blind who have been unable to study
his works. This curiosity to see the man himself dis-
pleases him. With a kind of outraged modesty he
withholds his private life from the public gaze. Seek
for the writer in his work and don't intrude upon a
decent man. Don't interrupt his work or disturb
him in the calm of contemplation. His work alone
belongs to you. Leave the anecdotes and the silly
chatter for those who like to depict a great man in
his slippers.

Is Mr Hardy at home ? The bell seems to die away
in some distant world, in the heart of the heaths, in
the wilderness of Egdon.

But the old man deputes a maidservant in cap and
apron to receive our card in the white porch. She
returns to bid us enter.

The " parlour " is empty when we both come in.
Fairly large and simply furnished, the room is
hospitable, comfortable and tranquil. Beneath the
gaze of the pictures which recall to life some of the
Wessex scenes enshrined in the master's work, one
feels that everything in the room conspires to evoke
an atmosphere.

Mrs Hardy is the first to appear. She announces
that her husband will be with us in a minute.
Slightly built, his neck somewhat emaciated, with
the worn, shuttered countenance of age, hermetically
lined at the corners of his mouth, looking almost
rustic in his brown suit, the old man stands before
us. His greeting is at once sober and cordial. For
all his eighty-seven years he is alert and upright.

His face is wrinkled, but fresh. The complexion mates well with those greyish-blue eyes of such piercing clarity. The curving aquiline nose confers upon the face an air of aristocratic aloofness, devoid alike of haughtiness and affectation. "That frail bird-like head, despoiled of its plumage," wrote M. Jacques Emile Blanche on 21st January, 1928, in *Les Nouvelles Littéraires.* And it is indeed the impression of a head from which the crown has been plucked that one always receives from that much-lined face, an impression that recurs in the sharply hewn bust of Mr Serge Yourievitch. The recollections of M. Blanche belong to 1904, but the description retains all its value.

Our immediate duty is to explain the motives of our visit, to say that we have come, not to pick up a few details, but to receive in the presence of the man and of his work, with their background of a whole countryside, a great lesson in humanity. Our words evidently arouse no alarm in the master, for a frank, almost impulsive conversation begins. To reproduce the note of familiarity which characterized the dialogue we must give the actual substance of these two interviews.

"Yes," says Thomas Hardy, "nothing irritates me so much as the mania of those critics who want at all costs to find something autobiographical in my novels and to identify me, for instance, with the character of Jude or Stephen. I assure you that nothing is further from the truth. The elements from which I have derived the idea of a novel are often manifold, sometimes strange and incongruous. Imagination and invention play a greater rôle than people realise."

" I have often had recourse to the same method when describing the surroundings, amid which the incidents in my novels were staged. A single scene is frequently formed from the synthesis of several sites. It is thus made up of original features borrowed from a number of different spots. I carried out this task of recomposition almost involuntarily. . . . It was simply forced upon me."

The master seemed unwilling to pursue these reflections. There were other topics on which his curiosity must be satisfied. . . .

He was evidently very anxious to know how France had fared since the war, to learn how the country looked with its features marred by invasion. Both he and Mrs Hardy seemed much impressed by the social changes noticeable in Great Britain since the years of blood. The master also spoke to me of his admiration for some of the prominent figures on the other side of the Channel. Among them was Anatole France, whom circumstances always prevented him from meeting, and we spoke of " M. Bergeret's " books and of the reception at that time accorded to them. The slow agony of La Béchellerie proved to be a kind of apotheosis. It would seem that the public had subsequently veered round. Works like those of Marcel Proust provoked its curiosity in different matters, thus directing its favour, no doubt only momentarily, from other writers.

These oscillations of taste interested Mr Hardy. " And Balzac ? " he inquired. That compact structure, I explained, retains all its solidity. It stands like one of those temples, assured of the tribute of its worshippers, no longer dependent upon fits of

enthusiasm or an occasional vogue. Did this move
the master of Max Gate to reflect how his work would
stand in twenty or thirty years' time, to try to en-
visage the damage wrought by the years ? At least
it seemed that his thought strayed from us for a
moment, to follow in contemplation this line of
development.

Though sparing in the gift of his friendship,
Thomas Hardy is not forgetful of those whom he has
not seen for a long time, such as the painter Jacques
Emile Blanche, whose two or three portraits of the
novelist are well known. The writer spoke most
sympathetically of his painter, recounting the whole
story of each canvas and even praising the artist's
pronunciation of English.

The patriarch of English letters does not like
lengthy periods. His sentences are short and in his
voice there is that note which one always encounters
among those who live in contact with the soil, less
abrupt than the intonation of the Londoner or of the
inhabitant of the great towns, a singing note, almost
a note of folklore.

Many of those who have spoken with him have
been surprised at the simple, narrative character of
his conversation. Hardy never aimed at being
brilliant or profound. He chats unconstrainedly,
passes without difficulty from one subject to another
and seems in quest of that humble jog-trot truth
which knows how to make its way in the world. He
makes ample provision for his poet's store-house from
facts gleaned here and there and often founds mighty
epitomes upon mere odds and ends of history and
anecdote.

We reverted to the war itself, to personal recollec-

tions, to our presence at a congress organised by
Norman Angell to discuss problems of war and
peace, held near Maidenhead on the very eve of the
catastrophe. On a morning full of anxiety we left
it in the company of Mr J. M. Robertson, discussing
the Serajevo episode. We returned to Cambridge
before going to Northern France, so soon to be in-
vaded. It seemed to me that the author of *The
Dynasts* found in events in which individuals were
moved about like chessmen (I read it in the attention
with which he listened to me), a catastrophe similar
to that upon which he had founded his epic, itself
a mere episode in the cycle of time.

"What can mere goodwill do at Geneva or any-
where else to prevent the inevitable recurrence of
war?" One felt that malignant powers lurked
behind the outer crust of things, that the full cycle
of Time was not yet accomplished and that, in the
eyes of him who had summoned up the vision of
Napoleon, the Immanent Will, murderous and destructive, would not lay down its iron sceptre of
tyranny to-morrow.

Once we were assembled about the tea and the
cakes dispensed by Mrs Hardy, the conversation
became less gloomy. The writer made merry for a
few minutes at the expense of the visitors who sought
to force an entry into his retreat and to take snap-
shots of his flower-decked lawns, with a view to
carrying away pansies which should transform the
rare editions of his works into the semblance of a
herbal.

His talk became quite racy in its animation when
he described the tempestuous arrival of his friend
Bernard Shaw in a car worthy of an ambassador,

coming all triumphant from Weymouth, where he had occupied the king's room in the best hotel.

It was now time to take leave. When should we next see Mr Hardy? We know that he approves of the way in which we have tried to study his work, without seeking to link it closely with biographical notes, the material for which he has always refused to supply. There is a note of encouragement which we do not deserve in the poet's farewell. The master expresses the hope that our labours will receive their reward.

But we also take with us some flowers from the garden of Max Gate, pink and mauve sweet-peas and some white roses. I shall always see the last gesture of farewell, brief but cordial, which Hardy bestowed upon me. It was in very truth farewell.

The cottage where Hardy was born is in the hamlet of Upper Bockhampton. One ascends a narrow road, bordered by houses standing at intervals amid the clumps of trees, dripping with the July rain. There it is, a few yards from that land of heaths and brambles and birch-trees, which has become a land of romance in the novelist's work. The sodden branches dry themselves against the humble thatch. On the side overlooking the dale there is an abandoned garden. The house seems empty, the only sound is the barking of a dog. The rustic façade is white-washed and buried under rose-trees and climbing plants. Branches and foliage droop about the door, to hinder access. It is an abode belonging to a past which has already disappeared, a sanctuary almost estranged from its purpose. It is only country houses that seem so utterly deserted and the doors must be

rattled for a long time and the windows well shaken
before its inmate can be induced to issue forth, as
from a mole-hill. She seems to emerge from a dream,
a legend from far-off days. One is tempted to believe
that the noise alone has roused her from nothingness
or awakened her from her lethargy. At last the door
opens under the shower of drops falling from the
rose-tree which masks it, and an alert-looking old
woman, speaking distinctly, but with a voice which
seems to come from the distance tells us that the
premises cannot be seen this morning.

There is no doubt an allusion to beds which are not
made and sweeping which still has to be done. We
are not seriously impressed by this housekeeper's
point of view. We want to see the walls, the rooms
which received the earliest cries of the future genius,
when that larva of human flesh first appeared in the
maternal chamber. The furniture made up of pieces
of different sets, the age of the chairs, the form of the
piano and the stagnant air seem to retain those impressions sometimes preserved in an old portfolio,
where the notepaper has not lost its character of
yearning and reverie. Yes, little as he himself realises
it, Hardy is held fast in these stones, even in this
clumsy rickety staircase which one climbs in fear and
trembling.

The old woman chatters and points things out.
The escutcheon over the fireplace represents the arms
of the Hardy family. The young architect no doubt
painted them during his holidays. The worthy
woman is the widow of a non-commissioned officer in
the Indian army. She has lived for a long time in
India, and it is warmer there than here, she says.

" Here was the . . . there he used . . ." We ask

her if she is not related to the poet. But no, she is
only the tenant of a Member of Parliament who has
bought the house and annexed it to his estate. Now
all the devotees of the work of Wessex come here on
pilgrimage and many are the obols dropped into the
little wooden box. In accordance with the English
custom one signs one's name in a book which is kept
as a register.

We feel Hardy everywhere in the house. The old
woman tells us that the illustrious old man often
comes for a quarter of an hour's stroll on the heath,
but she admits that he never comes in and seems to
avoid the little garden now no longer recognizable.

" Have you read Mr Hardy's books ? "

" Oh, no, sir; my son told me that they would be
too depressing for me."

A wondrous answer, which, in its profound irony,
might be for the poet the source of one of these cruel
little pieces in the *Satires of Circumstance* and *Time's
Laughingstocks.*

" Then, you cultivate your garden ? "

" A little, sir, for the animals—the rats, the rab-
bits and the pheasants—come and eat our fruit and
vegetables and don't leave us much."

Farewell, thatch, lost amid the foliage. Let us
bend over the yellow flowers which adorn the village
border. At thy feet are buttercups of an unknown
kind, " pampas buttercups " . . . and these ranun-
culus, they too certainly do not date from Hardy's
childhood.

July 1927,

APPENDIX III

A

HARDY gave free expression to his views on marriage and the education of the sexes in the course of two enquiries into these questions undertaken by two periodicals. In *Hearst's Magazine* of June 1912 Hardy replied: "I can only suppose, in a general way, that a marriage should be dissolvable at the wish of either party, if that party prove it to be cruelty to him or her, provided (probably) that the maintenance of the children, if any, should be borne by the breadwinner."

In May 1894 he had already expressed himself with great frankness on the question of sexual education, in the *New Review* in the course of another enquiry of a similar character. He begins by saying: "A girl should certainly not be allowed to enter into matrimony without a full knowledge of her probable future in that holy state, and the possibilities that may lie in the past of the elect man."

Hardy shows himself a resolute partizan of telling the truth in the education of the sexes: "A plain handbook on natural processes specially conceived should be placed in the daughter's hand, later a similar information on morbid contingencies. Inno-

cent youths should, I think, also receive the same
instruction, for (if I may say a word but of my
part) it has never struck me that the spider is invariably male and the fly invariably female."

The writer does not allow prejudices to cause him
embarrassment. In his eyes, marriage does not
always appear a desirable goal for a woman, and he
sets on record the failure of our civilization, so
advanced in other spheres, but hitherto incapable of
finding a " satisfactory scheme for the conjunction
of the sexes."

B

Hardy would not, perhaps, have repudiated this
comparison with Nietzsche. In the *Manchester
Guardian* of 12th October 1914 he wrote in fact in
regard to Nietzsche :

" I need hardly add that with many of his sayings
I have always heartily agreed. . . ."

It is not impossible to show where the frontiers of
the two spirits touched.

Between Schopenhauer and Hardy, as between
Schopenhauer and Nietzsche, stands Darwin, the
channel whereby meliorism, the idea of the greatest
possible enriching and perfecting of life, reaches the
poet of *The Dynasts* and the hero of *Zarathustra*.
Life, therefore, may become its own aim, whereas
Schopenhauer stopped short with the denial of any
final aim.

APPENDIX IV

1840—2nd June. Birth of Thomas Hardy at Upper Bockhampton, near Dorchester, a market-town appearing in the novels as " Caster-bridge."

1865—*How I built myself a House. Chambers's Journal.*

1871—*Desperate Remedies.*

1872—*Under the Greenwood Tree.*

1873—*A Pair of Blue Eyes.*

1874—*Far from the Madding Crowd.*

1876—Hardy marries Miss Emma Lavinia Gifford.

—*The Hand of Ethelberta.*

1878—*The Return of the Native.*

1880—*The Trumpet Major and Robert, his brother.*

1881—*A Laodicean, or the Castle of the De Stancys.*

1882—*Two on a Tower.*

1883—*The Romantic Adventures of a Milkmaid.*

1885—Hardy constructs his house " Max Gate " at Dorchester, according to plans designed by himself.

1886—*The Mayor of Casterbridge.*

210

1887—*The Woodlanders.*

1888—*The Wessex Tales.*

1891—*Tess of the d'Urbervilles.*

1891—*A Group of Noble Dames.*

1892—*The Well-Beloved.*

1893—*Life's Little Ironies.*   A set of tales.

1894—*Jude the Obscure.*

1898—*Wessex Poems.*

1901—*Poems of the Past and the Present.*

1903—1908—*The Dynasts.*   A drama of the Napoleonic Wars, in 3 parts, 10 acts and 130
scenes.

1912—Death of Mrs Hardy.

1914—*Satires of Circumstance.*

—Hardy marries a second time, espousing the
writer Miss Florence Emily Dugdale.

1917—*Moments of Vision.*

1922—*Late Lyrics and Earlier.*

1923—*The Famous Tragedy of the Queen of Cornwall at Tintagel in Lyonnesse.*   A new
version of an old play.

—Visit of the Prince of Wales to " Max Gate."

1925—*Human Shows.*   Far fantasies, songs and
trifles. Life and Art by Thomas Hardy.
Essays, notes and letters collected for the
first time by Ernest Brennecke, jr., Greenberg, New York.

1928—11th January, 9.5 p.m. The great poet passes
away peacefully at " Max Gate."

APPENDIX V

BIBLIOGRAPHY

A—GENERAL WORKS

The Development of the English Novel. Wilbur L. Cross. Macmillan & Co. (1899).

Les Romanciers anglais contemporains. Y. Blaze de Bury. Perrin et Cie. (1900).

The Victorian Age in Literature. G. K. Chesterton. Williams & Norgate (1913).

L'Angleterre Moderne, Son Evolution. Louis Cazamian. Flammarion (1916).

Le Roman Anglais de notre Temps. Abel Chevalley. N.R.F. (1921).

Le Roman et les Idées en Angleterre. Madeleine Cazamian. Istra Strasbourg (1921).

La Femme Anglaise au XIXe siècle et son Evolution, d'après le roman anglais contemporain. Léonie Villard. Didier (1920).

The Beardsley Period. Osbert Burdett. John Lane (1924).

L'Influence du naturalisme français sur les romanciers anglais de 1805 à 1900. W. C. Frierson. Marcel Giard (1925).

212

A Century of the English Novel. Cornelius Weygandt. Brentano's Ltd. (1926).

Sex Expression in Literature. V. E. Calverton. Boni & Liveright (1926).

Dickens et la France. Floris Delattre. J. Gamber (Chap. Le Roman de Dickens et le Naturalisme français) (1927).

B—WORKS DEVOTED TO THOMAS HARDY

The Art of Thomas Hardy. Lionel Johnson. Lane (1894).

Thomas Hardy, Penseur et Artiste. F. A. Hedgcock. Hachette (1911).

Thomas Hardy, an illustration of the philosophy of Schopenhauer. Helen Garwood. Winston, Philadelphia (1911).

Thomas Hardy. A critical study. Lascelles Abercrombie. Martin Secker (1912).

Thomas Hardy. Harold Child. Nisbet & Co. (1916).

La Femme dans le Roman de Hardy. A. Liron. Didier (plaquette) (1919).

Thomas Hardy. A Study of the Wessex Novels. H. C. Duffin. Longmans (1916). Republished in 1921 with an appendix devoted to the poet and to *The Dynasts.*

Thomas Hardy, Poet and Novelist. Samuel C. Chew. Longmans (1921).

Thomas Hardy, The Artist, the Man and the Disciple of Destiny. A. Stanton Whitfield. Grant Richards (1921).

The Technique of Thomas Hardy. J. W. Beach. University of Chicago Press (1922).

Thomas Hardy's Universe. A study of a poet's mind. Ernest Brennecke, jr. T. Fisher Unwin, London (1924).

Character and Environment in the Novels of Thomas Hardy. H. B. Grimsditch. Witherby, London (1925).

The Life of Thomas Hardy. Ernest Brennecke, jr. Greenberg, New York (1925).

Talks With Thomas Hardy, at Max Gate (1920-1922). Vere H. Collins. Duckworth (1928).

Thomas Hardy From Serial to Novel. Mary Ellen Chase. University of Minnesota Press (1928).

Hardy and his Philosophy. Patrick Braybrooke. Daniel (1928).

Le Message de Thomas Hardy. Gerard de Catalogne. Cahiers d'Occident (1928).

Thomas Hardy, Dictionary. F. Outwin Saxelby. Routledge (1911).

A Bibliography of the Works of Thomas Hardy, 1865-1915. A. P. Webb. Hollings (1916).

C—WORKS DEVOTED TO THE WESSEX NOVELS

Thomas Hardy's Wessex. Herman Lea. Macmillan (1925).

The Hardy Country. C. G. Harper. Black (1925).

D—STUDIES AND ARTICLES

" Tess of the d'Urbervilles." *Longman's Magazine,*
Nov. 1892 (Andrew Lang), republished in a
selection of critical works, *Notorious Literary
Attacks,* edited by Albert Mordell. Boni &
Liveright (1926).

Les Marges (1903-1908). *Réflexions à propos de
Thomas Hardy.* Eugène Montfort. Les Marges
(1903).

Essays on Poetry. " Mr. Hardy's old age." J. C.
Squire. Hodder & Stoughton.

Le Roman anglais contemporain. Firmin Roz
(" Etude sur Thomas Hardy."). Hachette
(1912).

Figures of Several Centuries. A note on the genius
of Thomas Hardy. Arthur Symons. Constable
(1917).

Some Modern Novelists. H. T. and W. Fowlett.
Holt & Co., New York (1918).

Essays on Modern Novelists. A study of Thomas
Hardy. William Lyon Phelps. Macmillan
(1919).

Aspects of Literature. The poetry of Thomas Hardy.
J. Middleton Murry. Collins (1920).

Studies in Literature. " The Poetry of Thomas
Hardy." Sir Arthur Quiller-Couch. Cambridge
University Press (1923).

Introduction de Jethro Bithell, à une traduction
française de *Poèmes de Thomas Hardy.* J.
Fournier-Pargoire. Les Marges (1925).

Ce vice impuni, la lecture. Valéry Larbaud. " Etude sur Thomas Hardy, dramaturge." Albert Messein (1925).

Les Nouvelles Littéraires. " Une heure avec Thomas Hardy." Frédéric Lefèvre (February 21st, 1925).

Revue Anglo-Américaine. " La fatalité intérieure dans les romans de Hardy." J. J. Mayoux (January-February 1927).

Some Diversions of a Man of Letters. " The Lyrical Poetry of Thomas Hardy." E. Gosse. Heinemann.

The Lamp and the Lute. Bonamy Dobrée.

E—SUPPLEMENT

Countless studies and articles appeared on the occasion of Hardy's death. Many were only obituary notices. The following may be noted :

IN FRANCE

Léon Daudet. *L'Action Française* (January 16th, 1928).

Edmond Jaloux. *Candide* (January 19th, 1928).

Gérard Bauër. " Le Cœur et les Cendres de Thomas Hardy." *Echo de Paris* (January 19th, 1928).

René Puaux. *Le Temps.* Two articles (January 13th and 17th, 1928).

J. E. Blanche. *Nouvelles Littéraires.* " Souvenirs de Thomas Hardy " (January 21st, 1928).

Louis Gillet. *Revue des Deux Mondes* (February 1st, 1928).

Abel Chevalley. *Revue de Paris* (February 1st, 1928).

H. D. Davray. *Mercure de France* (February 15th, 1928).

Le numéro d'Hommage de la *Revue Nouvelle* (contributions de MM. Middleton Murry, James Joyce, Eden Phillpotts, René Boylesve, Marcel Proust, Jean Schlumberger, Ramon Fernandez, J. L. Vaudoyer, G. D'Hanghest, Franz Hellens, Edmond Jaloux, Pierre d'Exideuil, Charles du Bos) (February 1928).

J. J. Mayoux. " L'Amour dans les Romans de Hardy." *Revue Anglo-Américaine* (February 1928).

IN ENGLAND

J. C. Squire. " Thomas Hardy." *The Observer* (January 15th, 1928).

The Times Literary Supplement. " Thomas Hardy's Novels " (January 19th, 1928).

The Times Literary Supplement. " Thomas Hardy, Poet " (January 26th, 1928).

Vernon Rendall. " Thomas Hardy." *English Review* (February 1st, 1928).

A. H. Garstang. " The Humour of Thomas Hardy." *The Fortnightly Review* (February 1928).

S. M. Ellis. " Thomas Hardy, Some personal recollections." *The Fortnightly Review* (March 1928).

John Freeman. " Thomas Hardy." *The London Mercury* (March 1928).

George King. " Thomas Hardy, Novelist and Poet." *The Cornhill Magazine* (March 1928).

IN THE UNITED STATES OF AMERICA

Mark van Doren. " Thomas Hardy, Poet." *The Nation* (February 8th, 1928).

H. M. Romlinson. " Hardy at Max Gate." *The Saturday Review of Literature* (February 11th, 1928).

FRENCH TRANSLATIONS

Le Trompette-Major, roman traduit de l'anglais par Yorick Bernard-Derosne. Paris. Hachette (1882).

Tess d'Urbervilles, roman traduit de l'anglais. Paris. Hachette (1901). Nouvelle édit: *La Sirène* (1914) (Traduction par Mlle. Rolland).

Jude L'Obscur, roman traduit de l'anglais par Firmin Roz. Paris. Ollendorf (1903). Nouvelle édit: *Albin Michel* (1927).

La Bien-Aimée, roman traduit de l'anglais par Eve Paul Margueritte. Paris. Plon (1909).

Deux Yeux Bleus, roman traduit de l'anglais par Eve Paul Margueritte. Paris. Plon (1913).

Une Femme Imaginative, nouvelle traduite de l'anglais par Georges Bazile. Les cahiers britanniques et américains d'aujourdhui, No. 2 (1918).

Les Petites Ironies de la Vie, nouvelles traduites de l'anglais par Mme. H. Boivin. Paris, Rieder, 2e édition (1920).

Le Maire de Casterbridge, roman traduit de l'anglais par P. H. Neel. Paris. Nouvelle Revue Française (1922).

Le Retour au Pays Natal, roman traduit de l'anglais par Eve Paul Margueritte. Paris. Flammarion (1923).

Sous la Verte Feuillée!, roman traduit de l'anglais par Eve Paul Margueritte. Paris. Flammarion (1924).

Poèmes de Thomas Hardy, traduction Jeanne Fournier-Pagoire. Les Marges (1925).

Poèmes de Thomas Hardy, traduits par Madame Maurice Denis. Revue Hebdomadaire.

IN COURSE OF PREPARATION

Jude L'Obscur, traduction intégrale. Madame F. Laparra. Paris. Stock. Le Cabinet Cosmopolite.

NOTE.—Our quotations refer to the text of the editions published by Macmillan & Co.